AIR VANGUARD 3

SOPWITH CAMEL

JON GUTTMAN

First published in Great Britain in 2012 by Osprey Publishing,
Midland House, West Way, Botley, Oxford, OX2 0PH, UK
44–02 23rd St, Suite 219, Long Island City, NY 11101, USA
E-mail: info@ospreypublishing.com

Osprey Publishing is part of the Osprey Group

© 2012 Osprey Publishing Ltd.

All rights reserved. Apart from any fair dealing for the purpose of private study, research, criticism or review, as permitted under the Copyright, Designs and Patents Act, 1988, no part of this publication may be reproduced, stored in a retrieval system, or transmitted in any form or by any means, electronic, electrical, chemical, mechanical, optical, photocopying, recording or otherwise, without the prior written permission of the copyright owner. Inquiries should be addressed to the Publishers.

A CIP catalog record for this book is available from the British Library

Print ISBN: 978 1 78096 176 7
PDF e-book ISBN: 9 781 78096 177 4
EPUB e-book ISBN: 9 781 78096 178 1

Index by Zoe Ross
Typeset in Deca Sans and Sabon
Originated by PDQ Digital Media Solutions Ltd, Suffolk UK
Printed in China through Bookbuilders

12 13 14 15 16 10 9 8 7 6 5 4 3 2 1

www.ospreypublishing.com

Osprey Publishing is supporting the Woodland Trust, the UK's leading woodland conservation charity, by funding the dedication of trees.

ACKNOWLEDGEMENTS

Andy Kemp, Colin A. Owers, Michael O'Neal, John Paloubis, Alan Toelle, Aaron Weaver, Mike Westrop and Greg Van Wyngarden for their assistance in preparing this volume. Posthumous thanks also to former Camel pilots Gerald A. Birks, David S. Ingalls, Donald R. MacLaren, Hardit Singh Malik, Leonard H. Rochford, George A. Vaughn Jr and Thomas F. Williams for their kind assistance in the course of the author's past research.

CONTENTS

INTRODUCTION   4

DESIGN AND DEVELOPMENT   4

TECHNICAL SPECIFICATIONS AND VARIANTS   13
- Sopwith Camel performance figures
- Flying the Camel
- Night Fighters and Comics
- A Camel (re)built for two
- Monoplanes
- Trench Fighter 1
- The shipboard Camel

OPERATIONAL HISTORY   32
- Western Front
- Italy
- The East
- Carrier operations
- Post-war Camels

CONCLUSION   61

FURTHER READING   63

INDEX   64

SOPWITH CAMEL

INTRODUCTION

When the average person hears about World War I in the air, among the first names that come readily to mind is 'Sopwith Camel'. Its iconic status may be somewhat exaggerated, but there is no question that the Camel was among the most produced, versatile and ubiquitous combat aeroplanes of its time, serving over land and sea from England to Mesopotamia, as well as post-war revolution-convulsed Russia. Camels sallied forth from frontline aerodromes to take on all opposition from Flanders to the Champagne. Night-fighting Camels and even more extensively modified Comics rose from airfields in England to defend its cities from bombing raids by Zeppelin airships, Gothas and Zeppelin-Staaken giants, while other Camels, acting as pioneering night intruders, tried to ambush them as they returned to their own aerodromes. Sopwith 2F1 'Ships Camels' shot up from carrier decks and towed lighters to engage enemy aircraft at sea – and in one case, to carry out a seaborne airstrike on an airship base.

Those who delve deeper into the Camel mystique – past its evocative name – find a curiously ambiguous attitude toward its flying characteristics. In stark contrast to its predecessor, the much-loved Pup, the Camel was described as a constant handful to fly, unforgiving and even vicious to the complacent and careless. Yet many of those who mastered its quirks revered the Camel as a breathtaking aerobat and a peerless dogfighter, and regarded themselves as something of a privileged fraternity, similar to pilots who got to take the controls of a Supermarine Spitfire in the next war.

The Camel was by no means the most aesthetically pleasing aeroplane to take to the sky in 1917. It was, however, among the most evocative of its era – and equally evocative of strong feelings from both its pilots and its adversaries. From its own era through the mists of time to the present, from dread to admiration, the one reaction that the sight, sound or image of a Sopwith Camel does not evoke is indifference.

DESIGN AND DEVELOPMENT

The line of fighting aircraft associated with Thomas Octave Murdoch Sopwith began with the Sopwith Tabloid, a sport aeroplane that seated two – a pilot to the left of his passenger – under the upper wing. A boxy looking but compact single-bay biplane of wood and canvas whose wing cellule was held together by cross-braced wire cables, the Tabloid commenced flight testing at Farnborough on 29 November 1913, wringing up to 92mph and a climb rate of 1,200 feet per minute out of its 80-hp Gnome rotary engine. Its performance won prizes on the racing circuit, and impressed the Royal Flying Corps (RFC) and Royal Naval Air Service (RNAS) sufficiently for both to order a single-seat scout version with a vertical stabiliser and rudder arrangement replacing the original, finless rudder in 1914. The Tabloid proved too light for the rigours of combat flying and was out of active service by the spring of 1915, but its basic configuration set the fundamental pattern for most Sopwith designs for the rest of the war.

Several Tabloid derivatives and some floatplane variants, the Schneider and the Baby, saw service and sometimes carried improvised armament in the war's first two years. Sopwith's first true fighting machine, however, was a two-seater that he co-designed with R.J. Ashfield and Herbert Smith, powered by a 110-hp Clerget 9Z rotary engine, and armed with a single .303 inch Vickers machine gun with Vickers-Challenger interrupter gear firing forward – later replaced by improved Scarff-Dobovsky gear in 1916 – and a .303 inch Lewis gun aft on a Scarff No 2 Ring Mounting. Named for its W-shaped cabane strut arrangement, the '1½ Strutter' was passed by the Sopwith experimental department on 12 December 1915. Although the airframe was just a more robust improvement on its predecessors, the 1½-Strutter introduced pivoting surfaces that could be moved upward against the airstream – early dive brakes – and a tailplane whose incidence the pilot could adjust in flight by a handwheel in the cockpit.

The RNAS was first to request the 1½ Strutter, deliveries beginning in February 1916, and the RFC was not long in following suit – another pattern that would be repeated with two subsequent Sopwiths. Licence-produced by French and Russian manufacturers as well as several British subcontractors, and powered by a variety of engines, the 1½ Strutter acquitted itself well as

A colourful array of Sopwith F1 Camels used by No 9 Sqn, Royal Naval Air Service, outside typical hangars at Middle Aerodrome, Bray Dunes, Flanders, during the autumn of 1917. (Les Rogers via Aaron Weaver)

French soldiers examine a Camel of No 28 Sqn, Royal Flying Corps, at Droglandt aerodrome in the autumn of 1917. (Les Rogers via Aaron Weaver)

both a two-place reconnaissance fighter and as a single-seat bomber, as well as, in later modified form, a single-seat night fighter in British home defence.

In the autumn of 1915 Sopwith produced a lightweight single-seater powered by a 50-hp Gnome rotary engine designed by test pilot Harry Hawker. Impressed by the sprightly performance of 'Hawker's Runabout', Tom Sopwith and his staff worked on a more robust military version to be powered by an 80-hp Le Rhône engine. Cleared for testing on 9 February 1916, the Scout, as it was officially called, impressed the Admiralty with its maximum speed of 110mph at 6,500 feet and climb rate of 10,000 feet in 12 minutes. What truly bowled over its pilots, however, was its combination of docile, well-balanced handling, tight manoeuvrability and good cockpit visibility, all in an aesthetically pleasing package that seemed to embody the far-from-ironclad adage, 'If it looks right, it flies right.'

Again, it was the RNAS that first ordered the Scout in April 1916, but upon reading a copy of the Admiralty's report RFC Maj Gen Hugh Trenchard pencilled in his own instant verdict: 'Let's get a squadron of these.' Another RFC officer, Col Sefton Brancker, is alleged to have observed a Scout alongside

A

SOPWITH CAMEL B3887 OF 2LT HARDIT SINGH MALIK, NO 28 SQN, OCTOBER 1917

A provisional reconstruction based on the combat report of the German who brought it down, which described the number '5' on its wing, this Sopwith-built Camel assigned to No 28 Sqn was flown by 2Lt Hardit Singh Malik, the first Indian to be commissioned an officer in the RFC, when he participated in an evening raid on Markebeeke aerodrome in foggy, rainy weather that his flight leader, Capt William G. Barker, had conceived and implemented over his squadron commander's head. Barker, Malik and 2Lt J. B. Fenton crossed the lines, only to encounter four Albatros D Vs of *Jasta* 18, whose pilots had had a similar idea. In the ensuing melee Fenton was wounded but escaped to Allied lines. Barker and Malik became separated and each had to fight his own way back, Barker claiming two assailants in the process, of whom Ltn Otto Schober crashed to his death at Sleyhage. After a difficult pursuit Ltn Paul Strähle drove Malik down with two bullets in his right leg, but Malik managed to cross Allied lines before force landing and Strähle's claim went unconfirmed. Malik rejoined 28 Sqn in January 1918, while the repaired B3887 also returned to service, with No 45 Sqn in Italy.

B5406

its two-seater forebear and exclaimed: 'Good God! Your 1½ Strutter has had a pup.' Despite official efforts to discourage it, the delightful new fighter soon became universally known by that name.

By the time the first Pups arrived at 'A' Sqn of No 1 Wing RNAS at Dunkirk in July 1916, the prototype of yet another Sopwith single-seater, powered by a 130-hp Clerget rotary, was joining them for frontline evaluation. Completed on 30 May 1916, Sopwith Triplane N500 combined the Pup's fuselage with three sets of narrow-chord, high aspect ratio wings that offered the pilot an even better view from the cockpit, as well as a climb rate and manoeuvrability even better than the Pup's. So capable was the Triplane that while flying N500 on 1 July Flt Lt Roderic Stanley Dallas of 1 Wing's 'A' Sqn drove a German two-seater down out of control south-west of St Marie Capelle – almost three months before Flt Sub-Lt Stanley J. Goble, in Pup prototype 3691, drove an LVG down out of control for that type's first success on 24 September. Six days after the Pup's first victory Dallas gained a second in the Triplane, driving an enemy scout down OOC. The Admiralty duly ordered the Sopwith Triplane, which it would use well into the fall of 1917, but while the French navy also fielded an *escadrille* of *triplan* Sopwiths, the type would see no service with the RFC.

In spite of their scintillating performance, Pup and Triplane pilots found themselves fighting at a disadvantage in the late summer of 1916, when the Germans introduced the Albatros D I and D II, whose twin synchronised machine guns collectively gave them nearly triple the rate of fire eked out of the single Vickers machine gun synchronised by Sopwith-Kauper gear that armed both Sopwith types. An extra gun required more power and in late August 1916 the Admiralty ordered a Pup N503, fitted with a 110-hp Clerget 9Z. That arrangement, however, only served to show that the Pup's airframe was not compatible with engines exceeding 100 hp.

Not one to rest on his laurels, Tom Sopwith, together with R.J. Ashfield, Herbert Smith, F. Sigrist and Harry Hawker, set to work on a completely new twin-gun fighter. On 22 December 1916, while Triplanes were fully equipping No 1 Sqn RNAS, the prototype Sopwith F1 was ready for flight-testing.

Aside from being a radial engine biplane the F1's family resemblance to the Pup ended there, for it had a shorter, deeper fuselage with the engine, cockpit and guns concentrated within the foremost seven feet. To facilitate production,

A Sopwith 2F1 'Ships Camel' takes off from a flight deck erected on the bow of seaplane carrier HMS *Pegasus* in the Firth of Forth late in 1918. A good, stiff headwind allowed Camels to alight from astonishingly short decks, though landing was another matter entirely. (Colin A. Owers via Greg Van Wyngarden)

Sopwith F1 N6346 was one of the earliest Camels to serve with Naval 4 Sqn at Bray Dunes and was flown by Flt Cdr G. M. Rouse in June 1917. (Les Rogers via Aaron Weaver)

Sopwith eliminated the dihedral on the one-piece upper wing and compensated by doubling the dihedral of the lower one, to five degrees. Short span ailerons were originally installed on both wings, but their length was increased on production aircraft.

A distinctive feature of the new aeroplane was a twin Vickers machine gun installation partially covered by a fairing that sloped upward from the nose, and was initially thought to protect the pilot from the slipstream effect sufficiently to make a conventional windscreen unnecessary. Since both guns had a right-hand feed, as early as 4 March 1917 reports came in of the symmetrical fairing making it virtually impossible to rectify a jam in the rightmost weapon, should it occur in combat. With that in mind, on 19 June Camel B2301 was tested with part of the front cockpit decking cut away to expose the right gun's breech, and on 28 July the RFC standardised that modification for operational aircraft in France.

Similar though it may have been in fundamental construction to its forebears, the F1's peculiar configuration gave it an appearance and flight characteristics that were equally pugnacious compared with the docile Pup and manageable Triplane. The first F1 was powered by a 110-hp Clerget 9Z engine when Harry Hawker got in its cockpit and, as he put it, 'bounced into the air' from Brooklands aerodrome on 26 December. The torque of the rotary engine, combined with the concentration of weight up front, endowed it with breathtaking manoeuvrability but Hawker noted the sensitivity of the controls, which required a judicious hand, especially during take-off.

Two subsequent unserialled prototypes were designated the F1/2, a naval prototype, and the F1/3, which was flown with the 130-hp Clerget 9B, 110-hp Le Rhône 9J and the experimental Clerget LS (Long Stroke), later rechristened the 140-hp Clerget 9Bf. It was allegedly when the latter was delivered to Martlesham Heath on 24 March 1917 that one of the Testing Squadron's pilots said, 'Just to look at the beast gives me the hump at the thought of flying it.' That remark, recorded by RFC technical officer Sir Harry Tizard, along with the gun fairing's appearance, led to the sobriquet 'Camel', which like 'Pup' was never official but nevertheless gained universal acceptance.

As the F1 developed, tapered wings with a single, plank-shaped interplane strut were tried, but when the so-called F1/1, powered by a 130-hp Clerget 9B was flown by the RFC Testing Squadron at Martlesham Heath in May 1917, the altered arrangement failed to yield the improved performance that Sopwith expected. One alteration that was adopted was a cutout in the upper wing centre section to alleviate the pilot's restricted view upward and forward – a significant weakness that would lead to enlarged apertures being made by Camel pilots in the field. The prototype's one-piece upper wing was also replaced by one built in three sections for production aircraft.

May 1917 also saw the second naval prototype, N518, test flown at Martlesham Heath with a new 150-hp AR 1 ('Admiralty Rotary No.1'), an improvement over the Clerget with steel-lined aluminium cylinders designed by RNAS engineering liaison officer Walter Owen Bentley. The engine's performance was so markedly improved that it was put into production as the Bentley BR 1, which powered the first operational Camels and became the best of their many power plants.

Also developed from the F1 were specialised naval variants. The FS1 'Improved Baby', a twin-float seaplane armed with a single Vickers gun and a supplemental .303 inch Lewis gun firing above the upper wing on a flexible

B

1. COOPER BOMBS AND CARRIER
Complementing the Camel's guns in the unpopular task of ground attack was a rack for up to four Cooper bombs that could be installed under the fuselage aft of the undercarriage. Upon release using a lever attached to a Bowden cable the bomb fell clear of the rack and the prong protruding down from the rack that prevented its five-bladed fan from spinning to arm it – to hopefully land on or reasonably near the target. Cooper bombs came in the form of the 20-lb Mark II-A, the 25-lb Mark II-B and the 49-lb Mark III.

2. ADMIRALTY TOP PLANE MOUNTING
Convinced that the 2F1 Ships Camel was most likely to encounter enemy airships and floatplanes at sea, the RNAS preferred a mixed armament of one synchronised Vickers and a Lewis firing over the upper wing or obliquely upward using the Admiralty Top Plane Mounting, a device rather more complex than the simple Foster rail mounting as used on RFC Nieuports, but which allowed the Lewis to be pulled down at an angle through the center section aperture by the pilot, who being seated directly under rather than behind the upper wing would not have been able to use the Foster mount. Likewise refecting the anti-airship role – valid, given the German use of Zeppelins in the reconnaissance role over the North Sea – 2F1 prototype N5 was also tested with eight Le Prieur rockets mounted on the interplane struts.

3. DOUBLE FOSTER MOUNT
The conception of the Sopwith 'Comic' was first tried in September 1917, when Capt F. W. Honnett, leader of A Flight of No 78 (HD) Sqn, had the controls of a Sopwith 1½ Strutter relocated to the observer's position and the synchronised Vickers gun replaced with an overwing Lewis on a Foster mount. The 1½ Strutters so modified were unofficially called 'Comics', but their night fighting performance was inadequate and in early 1918 they were replaced with Camels, some of which were likewise modified with twin Lewis guns on double Foster mounts and the pilot's seat moved back to where the fuel tank would normally be (it was repositioned in front of him). This arrangement prevented the gun flash from blinding the pilot at night, as would the Vickers guns mounted directly in front of him, and gave him the option of angling them upward at up to 45 degrees. Although 'Comic Camels' did yeoman service in Home Defence during the Gotha and R-plane raids of 1918, they were not used by the night fighter units stationed in France.

4. TWO-SEAT TRAINER CONVERSION
In response to the great many training accidents, often fatal, that were attributable to student pilots failing to simultenaeously master the procedures necessary to control the rotary engine and the Camel's flight characteristics, many officers at training establishments carried out their own conversions of Camels to two-seater configuration by replacing the main fuel tank with a rear seat and dual controls, and installing a small gravity tank in front of the forward cockpit. Some 24 such conversions are known to have been made, and were credited with reducing the accident rate at the schools that employed them.

1

2

3

4

mounting that allowed it to be pulled down for reloading to be fired upward, failed to find favour. However a land-based version of that design, designated the 2F1, did get a production contract. Also known as the Ships Camel, the 2F1 featured shorter-span wings and a narrower undercarriage track than the F1, as well as a hinged, folding tail for shipboard storage and slim steel tube cabane struts.

Aside from a brief appearance by F1 prototype N517 at the RNAS station at Dunkirk in March 1917, the first Camels to reach France arrived at Dunkirk on 17 May 1917. On the 25th N6332 was transferred to the RFC as an introductory sample for the production models that would be reaching No 70 Sqn in mid-June.

In early June 1917 No 4 Sqn RNAS began replacing its Pups and on the 4th Flt Lt Alexander M. Shook, piloting Camel N6347, attacked an enemy aeroplane 15 miles off Nieuport, which dived and escaped in a dense sea haze. Engaging 15 German aircraft between Nieuport and Ostende the next day, Shook sent a scout crashing on the beach and drove a two-seater down out of control 10 minutes later. The first frontline loss occurred on 13 June when Flt Sub-Lt Langley F.W. Smith, an American volunteer with eight victories previously scored in Pups, was killed in N6362. Some witnesses said his Camel broke up while he was stunting above the German aerodrome at Neumünster.

The Camels of Naval 4, joined by those of Naval 3, chalked up several more successes in June and July. On 10 July, however, Flt Sub-Lt E. W. Busby was killed in action and two days later Naval 4 was reminded of the new aeroplane's unforgiving nature when Flt Sub-Lt Sydney E. Ellis, a Canadian with two victories in Pups and three in the Camel, fatally spun into the ground.

Generally the Camel had enjoyed a good first month, but not without problems arising. Aside from the aeroplane's inherent tail-heaviness and need for perpetual vigilance while flying it, the mechanical Kauper interrupter gear proved to be defective and pilots were not keen on the gun-firing control, which at first was not located in the control column. Performance left something to be desired and RFC squadrons using the 130-hp Clerget 9B engine never found it satisfactory.

Camels equipped with the 150-hp Bentley BR 1 arrived at No 3 Sqn RNAS late in June and Flt Sub-Lt Leonard H. Rochford flew it for the first time on the 28th. 'It was an unstable machine and the powerful engine gave it a vicious kick to the right as soon as it was airborne which had to be corrected by using a lot of left rudder,' he recalled. 'However, no aeroplane could be manoeuvred so quickly and that was its great advantage in combat. During the several hundred hours I flew the Camel in France, I never met a German fighter that could outclimb me though some of them were faster on the level and in a dive. None could out-manoeuvre the Camel.'

On 9 December 1917 General Trenchard demanded that as many RFC Camel squadrons as possible convert to the 110-hp Le Rhône 9J engine, which is known to have been used on aircraft of Nos 3 and 46 Sqns, as well as the 17th Aero Sqn, a US Army Air Service (USAS) unit attached to 65 Wing, RAF, in 1918 (its sister unit, the 148th Aero Sqn, had Clerget-engined Camels). It is interesting to note, however, that the RNAS had comparatively few of the engine problems that cropped up in the RFC, since most of its Camels used the Bentley BR 1. In addition to the parent Sopwith Aviation Co. Ltd, F1 Camel airframe production was pursued by seven sub-contractors: Boulton & Paul Ltd, British Caudron Co. Ltd, Hooper & Co. Ltd, March, Jones & Cribb Ltd, Nieuport & General Aircraft Ltd, Portholme Aerodrome Ltd and Ruston,

Proctor & Co. Ltd. Production of 2F1 Ships Camels was undertaken by Sopwith (52, including the two prototypes), William Beardmore & Co Ltd (140), Arrol, Johnston Ltd (50), Clayton & Shuttleworth (25) and Hooper (contracted for 50, but only one, N8159, known to have been completed). As of 31 October 1918, the Royal Air Force had 2,548 F1 Camels and 129 2F1 Ships Camels on charge, 916 of which were in France or Italy, 181 in Home Defence units and 112 2F1s distributed aboard Royal Navy ships. By the time production ceased in June 1919, a grand total of 5,695 Camels were built.

TECHNICAL SPECIFICATIONS AND VARIANTS

The Sopwith Camel's fabric-covered wire-braced wood structure was well established long before it was conceived and was as straightforward as its development. The key to its distinctive performance was the concentration of weight and power within seven feet of forward fuselage, and it used a number of motor types, experimental and operational, to provide that power.

By the end of 1917, a total of 3,450 Camels had been ordered and 1,325 had been delivered to the services. During that time 1,546 Clerget and 540 Le Rhône engines passed inspection for use, an additional 875 Clergets and 1,314 Le Rhônes of French manufacture had also arrived, and the first 269 Bentley BR 1s had been built.

The BR 1, or 'Bentley Rotary', had originally been developed in the summer of 1916 in response to an Admiralty request to replace the licence-built Clerget 9B with an engine less prone to overheating, at a per-unit cost less than the Clerget's 907 pounds 10 shillings. Ostensibly basing his design on the Clerget – but in practice only employing its camshaft – Walter Owen Bentley incorporated his penchant for using aluminium alloy cylinders with cast iron linings and aluminium pistons to reduce weight, with a piston stroke of 6.7 inches (17cm). He also made use of dual ignition, with two spark plugs per cylinder, for reliability. The result, initially called the 'Admiralty Rotary' (AR 1), but later renamed the 'Bentley Rotary', indeed proved superior to the Clerget and once in production the cost per engine was 643 pounds 10 shillings.

In July 1917 both the 140-hp Clerget 9Bf and 150-hp Bentley BR 1 engines were tested with different compression ratios in an attempt to wring more output from them. Testing at Martlesham led to a Clerget with a higher ratio of 5.29 to 1 that became standard for Camels thereafter. Of five such variations tested on the BR 1, the best results came from installing larger induction pipes with a 2mm hole bored into the top casing of each. The result was a compression ratio of 5.7 to 1 and 11 more horsepower.

In early July 1917 Naval 3 began experiencing engine seizures in its BR 1 powered Camels, a malfunction that was traced to broken coil springs in the Bentley engine's oil pump. The CO, Wing Cmdr Redford H. Mulock, chanced to be at Dunkirk when W. O. Bentley was visiting.

'He met W. O. Bentley at Dunkirk and told him about our oil pump troubles,' Leonard Rochford wrote. 'Later he brought "W. O." out to Furnes and showed him the broken springs which had been kept for his inspection. "W. O." took them back to England with him and, not very long afterwards, returned to Furnes with a supply of springs made of a different material. Every engine in the squadron had its oil pump taken apart and the new springs fitted to it. We had no more trouble.

A close-up of the tail of restored F1 Camel B6291, now owned by the Javier Arango Collection at Paso Robles, California, showing the control cables. (Jon Guttman)

'Lieutenant W. O. Bentley RNVR had done us a very good turn and we were therefore sorry to hear later that, as the result of doing so, he had been reprimanded for "short-circuiting" officialdom instead of using "the usual channels". Such unofficial methods could sometimes save lives in wartime.'

In spite of the BR 1's superiority, enough simply could not be produced to completely eclipse the Clerget; in fact, other engines were needed to keep up with airframe production, resulting in a different Camel power plant for each squadron. On 31 October 1918 the RAF had 385 BR 1 powered Camels, 1,342 powered by Clergets and 821 with Le Rhône or 150-hp Gnome Monosoupape engines. The latter, first tested on a Camel at Martlesham in December 1917, featured dual ignition and a multi-position ignition switch that enabled it to run on nine, seven, five, three or one cylinder.

Although the Gnome's performance figures compared well with the BR 1's, it was not adopted for British use. When the United States Army Air Service (USAS) bought a consignment of Camels, it also bought a number of Gnomes for them, but Boulton & Paul's attempt to install the engines on its Camel airframes was brief and unsuccessful.

The standard price of an F1 airframe, excluding guns and instruments, was quoted at 874 pounds sterling, 10 shillings, while a 2F1 cost £825. The Clerget power plant cost more – 907 pounds 10 shillings – but the Le Rhône was less at £771.10 and the BR 1 a relative bargain at £643.10.

Sopwith Camel performance figures

Aircraft	F.1/1	B2512	F.1/3	B3829	N518
ENGINE	130 hp Clerget	130 hp Clerget	140 hp Clerget 9BF	110 hp Le Rhône	150 hp BR 1
Weight (lb)					
Empty	950	962	–	–	977
Loaded	1,482	1,482	1,452	1,422	1,508
Max. Speed (mph)					
At 6,500 ft	–	108	–	–	116.5
At 10,000 ft	112.5	104.5	–	108.5	111
At 15,000 ft	106	97.5	113.5	111.5	103
Climb to (minutes/seconds)					
6,500 ft	6/00	6/40	5/00	5/10	5/30
10,000 ft	10/35	11/45	8/30	9/10	9/50
15,000 ft	21/5	23/15	15/45	16/50	20/00
Service ceiling (ft)	19,000	18,500	24,000	24,000	18,500
Endurance (hours)	2¾	–	–	–	2½

The undercarriage of Camel B6291 at Paso Robles, showing details of the bracing cables and bungee cords. (Jon Guttman)

Aircraft	B3835	B3811	USAS Camel	F6394
Engine	150 hp BR 1 (5.7:1 compression ratio)	100 hp Gnome Monosoupape	150 hp Gnome Monosoupape	170 hp Le Rhône
Weight (lb)				
Empty	–	882	–	1,048
Loaded	1,470	1,387	1,523	1,567
Max. Speed (mph)				
At 6,500 ft	–	–	–	–
At 10,000 ft	121	110.5	117.5	113
At 15,000 ft	114.5	102.5	107	108.5
Climb to (minutes/seconds)				
6,500 ft	4/35	6/50	5/50	5/30
10,000 ft	8/20	11/50	10/20	9/35
15,000 ft	15/55	23/15	19/40	17/30
Service ceiling (ft)	22,000	18,500	21,500	21,500
Endurance (hours)	2½	2¾	2¼	–

The F1 Camel had a wingspan of 28 feet, a chord of 4 feet 6 inches and a wing area of 231 square feet. The four ailerons had an area of 9 square feet each, the tailplanes were 14 square feet, the elevators 10.5 square feet, the vertical stabiliser 3 square feet and the rudder 4.9 square feet. The 5-foot wing gap at the fuselage diminished at the wingtips, due to the 5-degree dihedral of the lower wing compared with none for the upper.

The Camel's overall length varied with its engine: 18 feet 9 inches with the Clerget; 18 feet 8 inches with the 110-hp Le Rhône; 18 feet 6 inches with the BR 1 or 150-hp Gnome Monosoupape; and 19 feet with the 100-hp Monosoupape or 170-hp Le Rhône.

Synchronisation for the F1's twin .303-inch Vickers machine guns also varied with the engine. For example, those using the 110-hp Le Rhône used a CC synchronising mechanism. This system had been designed by Major George E. Colley and George Constantinesco, a Romanian physicist who had come to England in 1910, and who had made a name for himself with his Theory of Sonics, now known as continuum mechanics, by which power could

Ruston, Proctor-built Camel B2487 'E' of No 65 Sqn RFC displays the underside Cooper bomb rack, which became standard weaponry from autumn 1917 onwards. Arriving on 28 November, it was flown by Lt C. B. Matthews to share in an Albatros D V OOC on 12 December. It was damaged by gunfire on 18 December, but on the 28th Matthews shared in driving a two-seater down smoking, followed by an Albatros scout destroyed the next day. B2487 went to a receiving park on 27 March 1918 and back to England two days later. (Stewart Taylor)

be transmitted by vibrations or pressure pulses in liquids, solids or gases. The CC gear applied Constantinesco's theory to a hydraulic system called Fire Control Timing Gear. First installed using oil as its medium in de Havilland DH 4s of No 55 Sqn in March 1917, the system was prone to chronic failure, but a later development, using a mixture of 90 per cent paraffin (kerosene) and 10 per cent oil, proved to be more reliable and in fact superior to mechanical interrupter gear, since it freed the gun's rate of fire from dependence upon the varying revolutions per minute of the engine.

Camels with 130-hp Clerget 9B engines used Kauper No 3 interrupter gear. Aldis ring and bead sights were standard on Camels, but individual pilots often replaced them with a variety of sights of their own choosing. In addition to its machine guns, the Camel could carry four 20lb Cooper Mark II-A or 25lb Mark II-B bombs in racks under the fuselage.

Late in 1918 Camels were flown at Orford Ness to test the feasibility of using the Guardian Angel parachute, a British variation on a German device that, although it only worked 50 per cent of the time, had saved a lot of *Flieger*'s lives that year. Major Oliver Stewart's report on 18 October, however, was less than encouraging:

'I flew a Camel, wearing a Guardian Angel parachute harness, and found that those movements of my body which would be required when fighting were restricted, and that on turning my head to look backwards and downwards, my chin came against the rings which go round the shoulders. The top part of the rings cut into my shoulders, causing me considerable discomfort, which was increased by any movement of the arm, such as that necessitated by altering the throttle and fine adjustment openings.'

Capt Reginald M. Charley had similar complaints the next day, adding that 'the strips and belt are over the harness, which means it cannot fit well, and the shoulder straps will always be liable to slip off.

'Another defect is that when a pilot is about to jump out with the parachute, he must first release his shoulder straps and belt, and it is most likely that they would be caught in the harness.'

Flying the Camel

Capt Ronald Sykes, who scored six victories in Camels with No 9 Sqn RNAS and 203 and 201 Sqns RAF, left behind useful memories of the procedures involved in getting the Sopwith fighter airborne and keeping it there. These,

Boulton & Paul-built Camel B9268, powered by a 110-hp Le Rhône engine, was assigned to a training school in England, for which purpose it is armed with a Hythe camera gun in place of the twin Vickers. (Greg Van Wyngarden)

written down for his pupils when he was serving as an instructor, were largely preserved in Chaz Bowyer's near-definitive 1978 work, *Sopwith Camel – King of Combat*.

Upon settling into the cockpit, the pilot ensured that both magnetic switches were off and that the petrol fine-adjustment lever was closed before turning the petrol tap on to 'Main tank'. 'Turn on the cock behind the air pump and hand-pump up to 1½ lb/sq in; at this pressure the relief valve should blow off', Sykes wrote. 'Open the petrol fine-adjustment by pushing the short lever for about one-half of its travel.

'Answer the mechanic's call of "Switches Off"; "Petrol On"; Suck in,' Sykes continued. 'While the propeller is being pulled round, move the long lever on the quadrant (controlling the barrel throttle-valve) a little way forward

C

1. SOPWITH F1 CAMEL B3889 'B1' FLOWN BY CAPT CLIVE FRANKLYN COLLETT, NO 70 SQN RFC, ERVILLERS, AUGUST 1917

One of the first Sopwith production batch, B3889 went to the RFC's first Camel-equipped unit, No 70 Sqn, and issued on 13 August 1917 to Capt Clive Franklyn Collett, the 31-year-old New Zealand-born leader of 'B' Flight, who destroyed a two-seater and an Albatros D V that same day, subsequently downing a D V down out of control on the 18th and destroying another on the 22nd. Flying other Camels, Collett brought his total to 11 with a triple victory on 9 September before being wounded by Ltn Ludwig Hanstein of *Jasta* 35. After recovery Collett became a test pilot, but was killed while flying a captured Albatros D V over the Firth of Forth on 23 December 1917.

2. SOPWITH F1 CAMEL B6499 FLOWN BY FLT SUB-LT HUGH B. MAUND, NO 10 SQN RNAS, TETEGHEM, DECEMBER 1917

Born in Hampstead, London, on 30 May 1896, but serving in the Canadian Expeditionary Force before serving in Nos 6, 12 and Sqns RNAS, Hugh Bingham Maund had scored two victories with 'Naval 10' by the time he received Sopwith-built Camel B6499, which – in striking contrast to sober RFC practice – sported one of the striped schemes applied in late November 1917 by the squadron's groundcrews in the interest of raising morale. Maund, whose plane also has the front white band extended over the fuselage turtledeck to signify his deputy flight leader status, had no successes in this machine before 1 April 1918, when Naval 10 was amalgamated into the RAF as No 210 Sqn and any remnants of its colourful markings removed, but he added another nine to his tally thereafter

3. SOPWITH COMIC B2402, CAPT GEORGE H. HACKWILL, NO 44 (HD) SQN, RFC, HAINAULT FARM, JANUARY 1918

Built by Ruston, Proctor & Co Ltd, B2402 was modified into 'Comic' configuration for Home Defence and as such was flown by Capt George Henry Hackwill, a former FE 2b pilot with No 22 Sqn with two victories to his credit, who after a stint as a flight instructor was assigned to No 44 (HD) Sqn as a flight commander. On the night of 28-29 January 1918 Hackwill, in concert with Lt Charles Chaplin Banks in B3827, brought down Gotha G V 938/16 at Wickford, killing Uffz Karl Ziegler, Ltn Friedrich von Thomsen and Uffz Walter Heiden of *Bombenstaffel* 14, *Bombengeschwader der Oberten Heeresleitung* 3. Hailing from Langtree, Devon, Hackwill later flew more conventionoal Camels in France as a flight leader in No 54 Sqn, raising his score to nine and receiving the Military Cross.

4. SOPWITH 2F1 CAMEL B7184, FLOWN BY LTN OTTO KISSENBERTH, *JASTA* 23B, EPINOY, MAY 1918

Among the multitude of aces who flew Camels in combat, *Jasta* 23b commander Otto Kissenberth may be unique, appropriating in April 1918 what is believed to have been Clayton & Shuttleworth-built, Bentley engined B7184, in which Flt Sub-Lt John E Youens of 3 Naval Sqn was brought down POW on 23 January. Remarking it in crosses and the *Staffel*'s black and white tail bands but retaining the original RNAS eagle fuselage marking, the German ace used it to shoot down an SE 5a over Tilly-Neville, for his 19th victory on 16 May, Lt S B Reece of No 64 Sqn surviving his forced landing in Allied lines. The Camel got revenge after a fashion when its engine packed up as Kissenberth was taking off on the 29th, causing him to crash from 40 meters height and injuring him for the rest of the war.

1

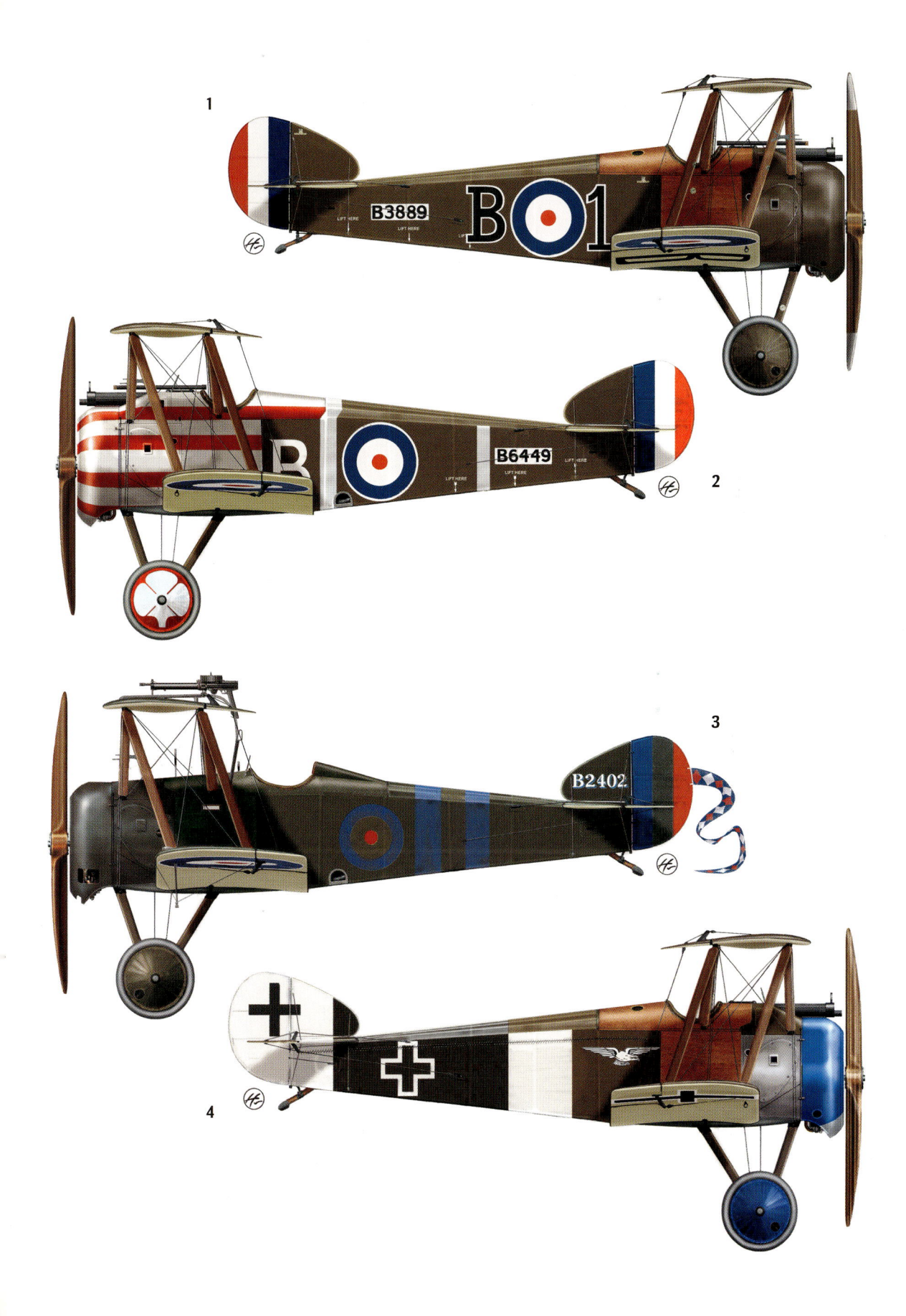

2

3

4

During a raid on Estourmel aerodrome on 20 November 1917, Clerget 9B-powered Camel B6385 'W' of No 3 Sqn RFC was brought down by anti-aircraft fire and its pilot, 2Lt T. J. Kent, taken PoW. During a test flight sometime thereafter, a German pilot fell victim to the Camel's unforgiving ways – at least providing a view of the fuel tank behind the pilot's seat. (Andy Kemp)

until a sucking, gurgling noise is heard as the petrol is drawn through the barrel throttle in the hollow crankshaft into the rotating crankcase. (The mixture passes through the crankcase and up the induction pipes to the overhead inlet valves.) While the propeller is being turned round, the oil pump will be drawing pure castor oil from the oil tank and forcing it onto the crankshaft bearings, timing gears, master and slave big-ends, and cylinder walls; all of which are being scoured by the petrol vapour, the castor oil being insoluble in petrol. After several turns of the engine the propeller is turned back to a position about "10 o'clock", then the mechanic shouts, "Contact". The pilot puts both switches ON, the petrol fine-adjustments lever nearly right back, the throttle half-open and replies, "Contact". The mechanic pulls the propeller down smartly; and in turn has his arm or belt pulled hard by the rigger to get him clear of the propeller as the engine fires.'

The Camel's 'hump' notwithstanding, the twin Vickers guns and sights rendered forward visibililty nil when it was on its tail, necessitating the pilot to peer sideways to ensure a clear take-off run ahead. Taking off on a grass surface required keeping the stick back to keep the tail from bouncing up. As the aeroplane accelerated the pilot of a throttle-equipped BR 1 powered aeroplane opened the throttle wide while moving the fine adjustment level just past the halfway position on the quadrant, determining by ear whether the cylinders were firing evenly.

'While the engine revs are rising,' Sykes advised, 'kick on plenty of left rudder to prevent a swing to the right. As speed increases push the stick forward and get the tail skid off the ground, high enough to give some visibility over the engine cowling. As the pressure on the stick rises, let it come back until the wheels leave the surface and the Camel flies off.'

After take-off ailerons were sluggish until the aeroplane had been flown level to reach a speed of about 100 knots, at which point they became sensitive. 'At all speeds between 70 knots and 150 knots the control response is precise and delightful,' Sykes added, 'although the elevator becomes much more sensitive at 150 knots.' Climbing involved pulling back the throttle and the fine adjustment lever every 1,000 feet, he said, 'otherwise the mixture becomes too rich and advertises the fact by leaving a trail of dark smoke behind, clearly visible for one's critics to observe!'

While making left turns the pilot was advised to use full left rudder to counteract the gyroscopic tendency of the engine to push the nose up;

Ruston, Proctor-built Camel B2402 is shown in its original configuration and 'B' Flight markings (a blue-white-blue band) with No 44 (HD) Sqn at Hainault Farm. (Les Rogers via Aaron Weaver)

conversely, full left rudder was again needed to counter the nose turning earthward. 'For climbing turns push the throttle and the petrol control forward to give maximum revs,' Sykes said. 'In fact, in all manoeuvres keep your left hand on the throttle levers and fly the Camel with your right hand on the stick.'

It may have been trying to master the Camel's manoeuvring idiosyncrasies while constantly working the throttle and fuel mixtures of its rotary engine that gave novices the most grief – and potential for disaster, and that was with the Bentley BR 1. The Clerget and Gnôme engines required a 'blip switch' to temporarily shut down or fire up various numbers of cylinders to achieve the speeding and slowing of revs that were achieved with relative smoothness with the throttle. The conversion of some Camels to two-seat trainer configuration helped student pilots tackle those skills separately, consequently reducing the percentage of crack-ups, but they were never used in sufficient quantities to make a significant difference throughout the services.

One of the many who expressed no regrets about learning to fly the Camel was Robert J. McLeod, a Canadian with No 3 Sqn RAF who loved to fly and who acquired great confidence in the aeroplane's flying ability early on in his training. 'It was fast, handy, got airborne quickly and had a phenomenal climb when properly rigged for it', he stated in a 1964 interview. 'At the Front, our machines were so rigged that we had to exert heavy pressure on the stick to keep its nose down. Hands off and she would loop forever, if you were good on the rudder. If not, she'd just rear up and flick over into a tight spin. You weren't supposed to take off in a climbing turn to the right, be we all did. Oh, it's true that you didn't want to doze off while flying a Camel; she kept you on your toes all right. That aeroplane would do anything a man could possibly ask of it, except fly in a very straight line upside down with the power on. Power on, upside down, she'd fly more in a sideways fashion than forward. She would glide very fine upside down with the power off, but the Camel was a fighter and was not supposed to fly in a straight line. We never flew straight and level, so that was just fine with us.

'She had a lot of strength, which was a big safety factor. You didn't worry about a Camel breaking up in the air. The only weak point was the engine, and I've flown with three blown cylinders. You wind up the engine too tightly and she'd start to disintegrate as 1,250rpm was supposed to be the maximum on the Le Rhônes.'

B2402 presents a striking difference in appearance after being converted to 'Comic' configuration, with the white in its markings subdued under a coat of camouflage paint. (Les Rogers via Aaron Weaver)

Night Fighters and Comics

The arrival of Sopwith Camels on the Western Front coincided with the start of a new wave of strategic bombing against Britain. With the decline in effectiveness in Zeppelin airship raids on English cities as the consequence of improved aircraft and interception techniques, on 25 May 1917 the first mass daylight strikes by long-range twin-engine Gotha G III and G IV bombers took place.

Britain's Home Defence (HD) squadrons were then equipped with a motley mix of second-line types and converted trainers, since there was an urgent need for the best aircraft at the Front. Nevertheless a handful of Camels were withdrawn to HD duty, and when 24 Gothas set out to attack London on 7 July, 95 aircraft took off piecemeal to oppose them, including five Camels. The only German loss of the raid occurred when Flt Sub-Lt J. E. Scott, in Camel B3774, caught up with a bomber 35 miles out to sea, fired 500 rounds into it and saw it dive into the water. When ten Gothas struck at Dover, Ramsgate and Margate on 22 August, Flt Lt Arthur F. Brandon in Camel B3834 sent one crashing in flames near Manston, for which he was awarded the DSC.

Although the Gotha units suffered more losses to accidents than combat, at the end of August the Germans switched to night operations, the first occurring on 3 September when four Gothas attacked the mouth of the Thames Estuary. Three Camels were among the 16 aeroplanes that rose against them and although Maj Gilbert W. Murlis-Green, Capt Christopher J. Quintin-Brand and Lt Charles Chaplin Banks sighted no raiders in the course of their 40-minute flight, they proved that, contrary to widespread belief, Camels could be flown at night no more or less safely than any other aeroplane with a competent pilot. Later that month No 44 (HD) Sqn at Hainault Farm, which had received its first Camels in August, became the first HD unit fully equipped with the type, for day or night interception operations.

Nocturnal missions involved taking off along two rows of cans holding lit oil-soaked rags, while landing was aided by Holt flares installed under the lower wings, though the danger of their igniting the doped fabric caused pilots to use them sparingly. The cockpit had a crude form of instrument lighting

A mixed bag of Camels and Comics of 44 Sqn line up for inspection at Hainault Farm. This was but one of several night fighter units providing home defence against the Gotha menace, although arguably the one whose exploits were most publicised. (Les Rogers via Aaron Weaver)

and in March 1917 Sgt A. E. Hutton of 39 (HD) Sqn devised an alternative to the useless ring and bead sight by piercing the ring sight and wiring a red electric light bulb in its stem, while the V-sight was similarly pierced to have three green lights at its extremities. In December 1917 this illuminated sight was superceded by the Neame sight, which added pre-sized rings to help the pilot determine target range.

To address the adverse effect that gun flashes had on a pilot's night vision, some Camels replaced the synchronised Vickers with a double Foster mounting that allowed twin Lewis guns to be fired over the upper wing. The upper wing cutout was enlarged to improve upward vision, the cockpit was set farther back to permit reloading, and the pilot was furnished with Hutton or Neame illuminated sights, as well as a headrest. As with the similarly modified 1½ Strutters before them, these specialised Camels were unofficially known as Comics.

Although the nocturnal Camels' presence was psychologically reassuring to the British public, a more material contribution proved frustratingly elusive until 18 December, when Murlis-Green, in Comic B5192, caught a Gotha G III of *Bombenstaffel* 15, *Bombengeschwader der Oberbefehlshaber des Heeres* (*Bogohl*) 3 near London. In spite of being temporarily blinded when an enemy tracer bullet struck his propeller, he managed to get a damaging burst into its engine. The bomber escaped, but subsequently ditched in the sea off Folkestone, Kent, where the pilot, Ltn d. R. Friedrich Ketelsen, died of injuries and the surviving crewmen, Obltn von Stachelsky and Geftr Wiesmann, used a self-destruct device to blow up the aeroplane before being picked up by a British trawler.

The Camels of 44 Sqn scored again on 28–29 January 1918, when seven Gothas and Zeppelin-Staaken R VI R39/17 attacked London and Kent. Capt George H. Hackwill in Comic B2402 and Lt C. C. Banks in B3827 caught Gotha G V 398/16 of *Bosta* 14/*Kagohl* 3 over Essex and their combined fire brought it down at Frund's Farm, near Wickford, killing Uffz Karl Ziegler, Ltn Friedrich von Thomsen and Uffz Walter Heiden. Camel HD units grew, but so did frustration in the succeeding weeks, to which was added tragedy on the moonless night of 7 March when Capts H. C. Stroud and A. B. Kynoch of 37 (HD) Sqn were killed in a mid-air collision.

The bombing campaign against England climaxed on Whit Sunday Evening, 19 May, when three Zeppelin-Staakens and 30 other bombers

The sole Camel retained by the 185th Aero Sq, USAS, after it replaced most of its Camels with SPAD XIIIs, sports a white post-war scheme and its squadron's bat insignia. The only night fighter unit in the AEF, the 185th fought less than a month attached to the 1st Pursuit Group, as much in ground attack as night patrol missions. It replaced all but one of its Camels with SPAD XIIIs shortly after the armistice. (Alan Toelle)

attacked and 84 defenders, including 31 Camels, rose to intercept. Maj Quintin-Brand in D6423 – a standard Camel to which he had allegedly added an overwing Lewis mount – closed on Gotha G V 979/16 of *Bosta* 18/*Bogohl* 3, and after two bursts caused it to explode into flames that singed his face, eyebrows and moustache, as well as the fighter's wing fabric. The raider crashed near Harty Ferry on the Isle of Sheppey, killing Vizewachtmeister Josef Jacob Arnold, Ltn Hans Gundelach and Vzfw Heinrich Heiligers. Quintin-Brand was awarded the DSO for his deed that night.

Meanwhile, Capt D'Urban V. Armstrong of 78 (HD) Sqn, operating from Sutton's Farm, repeatedly attacked a Gotha G IV of *Bosta* 18/*Bogohl* 3 until his ammunition was expended. His quarry was subsequently shot down in flames over the Roman Road at East Ham by Lt Anthony J. Arkell and 1AM Albert T. C. Stagg in Bristol F 2B Fighter C4636 of 39 (HD) Sqn. The German gunner, Geftr Wilhelm Schulte, was found dead in the bomber. The pilot, Vzfw Hans Thiedke, and observer Ltn Paul Sapkowick, opted to jump to their deaths from the burning aeroplane.

Fewer than half of the bombers returned unscathed from the Whit Sunday raid, effectively ending the Gotha threat to Britain. On 12 June, however, No 151 Sqn was formed at Hainault Farm from Camel flights drawn from 48, 78 and 112 Sqns. Placed under the command of Maj Murlis-Green, it was sent to France to use its fighters in a more offensive role – escorting FE 2b night bombers of No 101 Sqn or ambushing German nocturnal raiders as they returned to their aerodromes, making it in essence the first night intruder unit.

Arriving at Fontaine-sur-Maye on 23 June, 151 Sqn had a change of command to Maj Quintin-Brand on 1 July and its first success was a Gotha brought down with a crewman wounded on 25 July by Capt Archibald B. Yuille. On 1 August the unit 'intruded' on Estrées and Guizancourt aerodromes, dropping 25lb Cooper bombs and strafing the facilities.

By the end of the war 151 Sqn was credited with 21 victories and five probables, four of which were scored by Quintin-Brand to raise his wartime total to 12, and another four to Armstrong, making him a five-victory ace. A notable double success came on the night of 10 August when Capt Yuille, in Camel D6573, spotted a large aircraft silhouetted in searchlights over

Abbeville. After firing five bursts into it he saw an engine stop and a fire break out in mid-fuselage, after which the giant bomber heeled over and crashed in flames at Talmas, in British lines. On the same night Lts C. R. W. Knight and J. H. Summers caught a bomber at 9,000 feet and sent it down burning. Yuille's victim was Zeppelin-Staaken R XIV 43/16 of *Riesenflugzeug Abteilung* 501, lost with its nine-man crew.

On the night of 15 September Capt F. C. Broome in D6102 saw a 'Giant' coned by searchlights, closed to minimal range and fired 500 rounds into the fuselage and engine nacelles until he saw it go down burning with 'tremendous severity'. His victim was Zeppelin-Staaken R VI 31/17 of Rfa 500 whose pilot, Ltn Ernst Wohlgemuth, ran down the fuselage urging his crewmen to take to their parachutes. He was the only survivor when the aeroplane crashed near Beugny, however, and he died of his wounds on 1 October. By 22 September 151 Sqn had accounted for seven smaller German bombers, marking its most successful week.

One other RAF night intruder unit, No 152 Sqn, arrived in France on 22 October 1918, but the war ended before it could see action. On the night of 22 October, however, Lt Col Harold E. Hartney, commander of the American 1st Pursuit Group, was undertaking a night flight in a Boulton & Paul-built, 160-hp Gnome-powered Camel assigned to his group's 185th Aero Sqn when he nearly collided with a Gotha G V. Hartney fired at the bomber, but his claim to have shot it down was never confirmed, although the Americans did find a bullet-riddled Gotha on the ground near Verdun nine days after the armistice.

Aside from that unofficial success, the 185th Aero Sqn spent most of October 1918 engaged in ground attack rather than its intended night fighting role. Its sole fatality occurred on the 28th when 1Lt George W. Ewing, returning from a patrol through ground fog that impaired his night vision, crashed south-west of Rembercourt aerodrome and was unable to extricate himself from his burning Camel, set afire by his underwing Holt flares. During a daylight strafe two days later 1Lt Elihu H. Kelton, in Camel F1430, got into a dogfight with a Fokker D VII that ended in his being brought down by Ltn Justus Grassmann of *Jasta* 10 and made a PoW.

An unusual addition to the 185th Aero Sqn's armoury was a 35mm single-shot cannon, firing a canister of 16mm lead balls, that was briefly tested on one of its Camels shortly after the armistice. More fearsome in appearance than in practice, the experimental gun was found to have a maximum effective range of about 50 metres and was swiftly abandoned.

A Camel (re)built for two

Given the disturbing attrition plaguing pilots training on the Camel from the onset, it may be curious that drawings for a dual control two-seat version were not proposed until early 1918, issued in July and approved in October. Meanwhile, some airmen were taking matters into their own hands. Maj Christopher Draper, CO of No 208 Sqn, described a two-seater devised with the unit's own resources, though it was intended to carry a rear gunner. Draper claimed the contraption made a few sorties over the lines before RAF officials learned of it and ordered it restored to its original configuration.

Back in England, sometime in 1917 Maj Hugh V. Champion de Crespigny, then commanding the 23rd Training Depot Station at Montrose, authorised a Camel's conversion into a two-seat trainer, with a second set of controls extended to the rather snug rear cockpit. The only other necessary alteration involved removal of the main petrol tank from behind the front cockpit and its replacement with a gravity tank in front of the cockpit.

Late in 1917 or early 1918 Lt Col Louis A. Strange DSO, MC, commanding the 23rd Training Wing at South Carleton, likewise authorised his repair section officer to convert Camel B3801 into a two-seater. A similar modification at Shotwick, B5575 had its cockpit simply cut back into a two-man 'bathtub'.

At least 24 two-seater Camels were produced before the armistice and were distributed piecemeal, but the units that had them reported a noticeable drop in training casualties. A major factor in transitioning to Camels for pilots accustomed to Avro 504s powered by single-speed Gnome monosoupape engines was learning to use the throttle and fine adjustment petrol control that

D

1. SOPWITH F1 CAMEL N6812 FLOWN BY LT STUART D. CULLEY, NAVAL AIR STATION FELIXSTOWE, AUGUST 1918

On 31 July 1918 Lt Stuart Culley successfully flew a wheeled Ships Camel from a towed lighter at sea – and on 11 August he put the experiment to practical application. Taking off from a lighter towed by destroyer HMS *Redoubt*, he ascended to 19,000 feet and shot down Zeppelin *L53* near Terschelling off the Netherlands coast. Culley then landed in the water alongside the lighter, whose crew recovered both pilot and plane. His Beardmore-built 2F1, N6812 is now preserved in the Imperial War Museum.

2. SOPWITH F1 CAMEL F6032, FLOWN BY CAPT WILL HUBBARD, NO 3 SQN RAF, VALHEUREUX, SEPTEMBER 1918

Will Hubbard of Leamington Spa, Warwickshire, flew ground attack as well as fighter missions in No 3 Sqn, becoming 'C' Flight leader and earning the Distinguished Flying Cross. His last Camel, F6032, was a rebuilt machine with a Le Rhône engine and displays a rare case of unit markings that did not change in the wake of the German offensive of 21 March 1918. Hubbard used it to destroy a Fokker D VII on 4 Setpember followed by an Albatros two-seater the next day and send a D VII down out of control on 29 October for his 10th victory – and 3 Sqn's last of the war.

3. SOPWITH F1 CAMEL D3328 'Z' FLOWN BY 2LT HOWARD C. KNOTTS, 17TH AERO SQN USAS, AUXI-LE-CHÂTEAU, OCTOBER 1918

Clayton & Shuttleworth-built D3328 had a Le Rhône engine, underwing racks for four 25-lb bombs, a large, three-piece windscreen and, typically for the 17th Aero Sqn, had the fabric of its upper wing centre section cut away for better visibility. A spare plane, it was being flown by 2Lt Howard Clayton Knotts on 9 October 1918, when the 17th Aero Sqn attacked a railroad north of Awoingt, and in an attack on road traffic on the Verchain road. During the latter mission, however, Knotts, with six victories to his credit, was brought down by ground fire and taken POW. While being taken to the rear he managed to set fire to seven Fokkers that were on the same train and narrowly avoided being shot for sabotage.

4. SOPWITH F1 CAMEL, SERIAL UNKNOWN, FLOWN BY 1E SGT MAJ JEAN VAN DER VOORDT, 11E ESCADRILLE, AVIATION MILITAIRE BELGE, LES MÖERES, OCTOBER 1918

Jean van der Voordt was photographed in this Camel, on which a provisional colour reconstruction is based. On 15 October Belgian fighters had a major clash with German naval *Jagdstaffeln*. Vizeflugmeistern Alexander Zenses and Karl Scharon of *Marine Feld Jastas* I, II and IV claimed a Sopwith Dolphin each over Roulers while Ltn z S Gotthard Sachsenberg claimed an unconfirmed Camel over Hooglede. The 'Dolphins' were more likely SPAD XIIIs of the 10*e Escadrille* flown by Lt Louis Robin, who dived out of the fight, and Adj Charles de Montigny, credited with a Fokker before he came down in Allied lines, dying of his wounds on the 30th. Of three participating Camel pilots of the 11*e Escadrille*, van der Voordt claimed a Fokker that dived straight into the ground for his sole victory, while Sgt Léon Guillon drove a yellow banded Fokker down OOC. Van der Voordt's opponent turned out to be Ltn z S Reinhold Poss, 11-victory ace and *Staffelführer* of *Marine Land Jasta* IV, who who was taken POW.

1

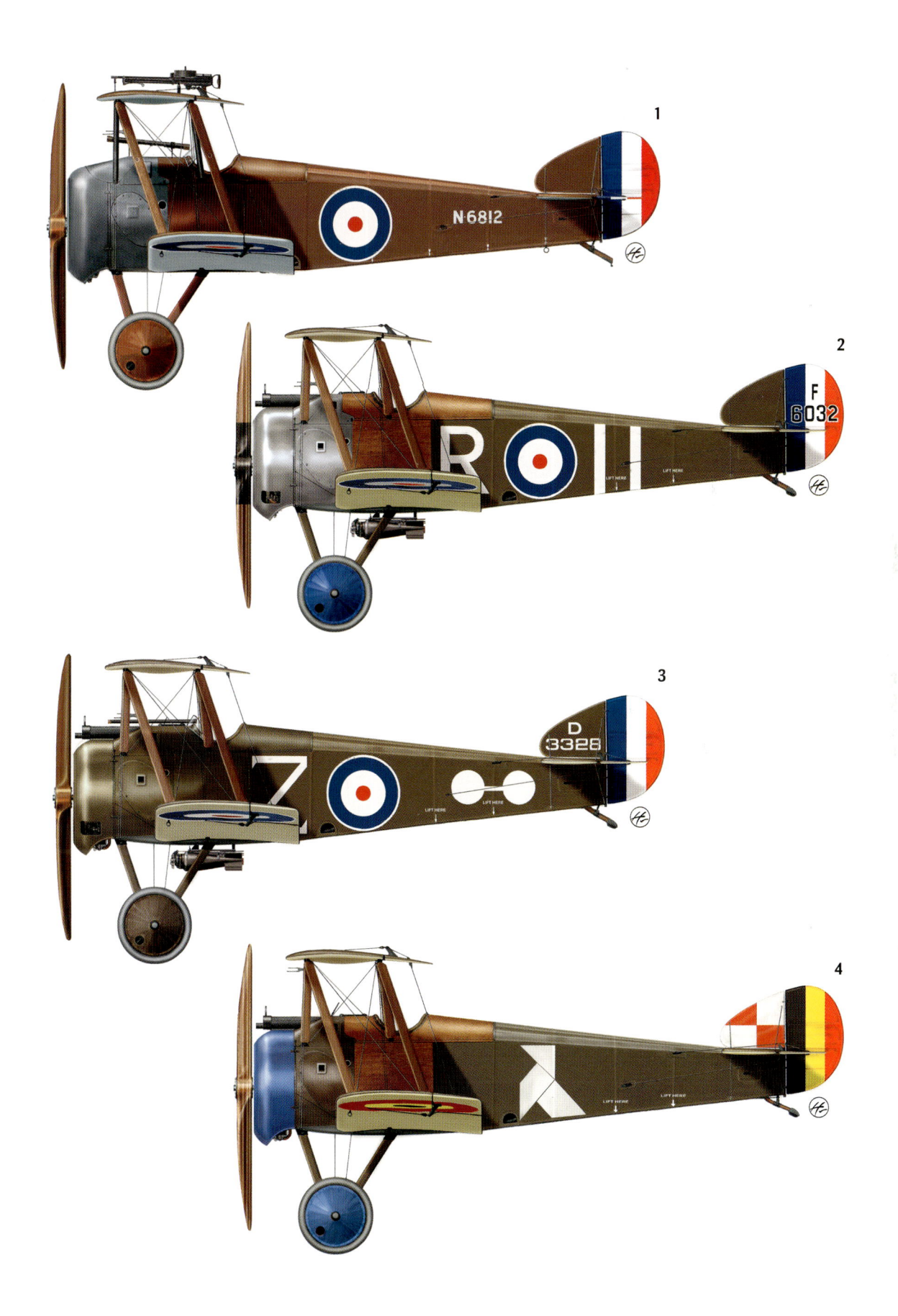

2

3

4

Camel C8368, built by March, Jones and Cribb Ltd, used a Le Rhône 9J engine and served with 189 Night Fighter Training Sqn at Sutton's Farm in October-November 1918, and subsequently No 78 (HD) Sqn until 27 May 1918. At some stage it was converted into a two-seat trainer, which must have been an invaluable boon to Camel trainees in night fighter operations. (Greg Van Wyngarden)

characterised the Clerget and other rotaries. Flying in a dual control machine with an instructor along gave a trainee the opportunity to master that change in engine control before tackling the Camel's flight characteristics.

Monoplanes

No 60 Sqn's unfortunate experience with Morane-Saulnier Ns, Is and Vs in the summer of 1916 left RFC commander Trenchard with an aversion for monoplanes that persisted throughout the war. In spite of that, Sopwith had a brief fling with monoplane versions of the Camel. The first, designated Sopwith Monoplane No 1, was an unarmed parasol designed for test pilot Harry Hawker's personal use, with the wing mounted an inch or two above the forward top decking by four struts and braced by wires from the fuselage underside and a pyramid of cabane struts above the wing. Appearing in the summer of 1918, its intent was reflected in its unofficial monicker, the Scooter.

Monoplane No 2, appearing in October 1918, was a more serious effort, with a wing of greater span and area – 28 feet, 10 inches and 160 square feet, respectively – longer ailerons and a 6-degree sweepback, mounted somewhat higher above the fuselage to accommodate two Vickers machine guns. The fuselage was that of Boulton & Paul-built Camel B9276, but the guns were wider apart and uncowled to improve the pilot's forward view.

The fact that the Swallow, as the newer monoplane was called, was powered by a 110-hp Le Rhône 9J engine, compared to the Scooter's 130-hp Clerget, suggests that it was not earnestly intended for acceptance and production, since at that very time the Sopwith Snipe biplane was entering service to replace the Camel. Rather, it was a testbed produced in response to reports of promising German parasol fighter designs such as the Fokker E V, which after having remedied wing structural problems experienced in August was just re-entering frontline service as the D VIII.

After trials at Sopwith the Swallow flew to Martlesham Heath on 28 October, but trouble with the fuel system delayed official testing until after the armistice. The subsequent RAF report, issued in May 1919, cited its performance to be inferior to that of a Camel with the same engine. That apparently killed the Swallow off, but the Scooter, under civil registration G-EACZ, enjoyed nine years of post-war racing and exhibition flying before finally being scrapped in 1927.

Trench Fighter 1

Arguably the 'dirtiest job' for Camel pilots since the autumn of 1917 was low-level ground attack, and in February 1918 Sopwith unveiled a 'trench fighter' designated the TF 1. Converted from Camel F1 B9278 and powered by a 110-hp Le Rhône engine, the TF 1 replaced its forward firing Vickers with two stripped Lewis guns fixed at an angle to fire forward and down through the cockpit floor, which was armoured from the engine compartment to the rear of the cockpit. A third Lewis was mounted above the upper wing centre section similarly to the naval 2F1.

After first flying at Brooklands on 15 February, the TF 1 was shipped to France on 7 March, but returned to Brooklands a week later and was promptly dismantled. Not only was the armoured aeroplane's general performance inferior to the standard Camel's – not surprisingly – but the downward-angled guns had already been proven less effective than the original forward-firing twin Vickers. In any case, Sopwith was working on a more specialised, higher-powered, armoured trench strafer, the Sopwith Salamander, whose prototype would arrive in France for service evaluation in May.

The shipboard Camel

When American aviator Eugene Ely flew his Curtiss Model D from an 83-foot wooden platform erected on the bow of the stationary light cruiser USS *Birmingham* in Hampton Roads, Virginia, on 14 November 1910, he set a precedent for navies around the world as far-reaching as Louis Blériot's 1909 Channel flight had done in regard to aviation in general. Lest there be any doubts about that, on 18 January 1911, he landed aboard a 133-foot platform on the armoured cruiser USS *Pennsylvania*, using a tail hook to catch one or two of 22 ropelines, their ends weighted with sandbags, each propped a foot above the deck. Fifty-seven minutes later, he took off again. Both ships were stationary at the time, but the Royal Navy, for one, grasped the possibilities. In 1912 it began a long and varied series of experiments with shipboard aircraft.

The Sopwith TF 1 turned out to be an interim ground attack concept that quickly gave way to the more specialised Salamander. (Jack Herris)

Take-off at sea proved to be relatively easy, even from platforms built atop gun turrets if the warship was heading into a brisk wind. Landings were the tricky bit, but on 2 August 1917 Sqn Ldr Edwin Harris Dunning alit his Pup on the foredeck of the converted 'large light cruiser' HMS *Furious* to enter the record books as the first aeroplane landing on a ship while underway. Tragically, while trying to duplicate his feat five days later a sudden updraft threw Dunning's Pup overboard and he drowned.

Tom Sopwith had been working on a shipboard fighter long before that. With the Camel successfully tested, he and his designers set to work on an 'improved Baby', originally conceived as a floatplane but ultimately taking form as a wheeled fighter based on the Camel airframe. The second prototype, N5, spent a short time on the Isle of Grain before arriving at Martlesham Heath for testing on 15 March 1917.

Although superficially resembling the original Camel, the 2F1, as the naval version was designated, differed in several respects, including a 13-inch reduction in wingspan due to a reduced-width centre section, the lower wing's dihedral increased slightly to 5 degrees 30 seconds, slim centre section struts made of steel tubing rather than wood, a narrower undercarriage track and a hinge that allowed the last 10 feet of fuselage to be folded for storage.

Most noticeable to the casual observer was the 2F1's armament, consisting of a single synchronised Vickers gun in the fuselage 'hump' and, initially, an unsynchronised .303 inch Lewis gun fixed above the upper wing. The latter arrangement was later replaced by an Admiralty Top Aeroplane Mounting, which elevated the weapon above the centre section cutout, but allowed the pilot to adjust the firing angle or pull the gun down for reloading.

An indication that the RNAS had Zeppelin hunting in mind even at that relatively late time could be seen in the eight electrically triggered Le Prieur rockets experimentally decked out on N5's interplane struts at the Isle of Grain in June 1917. Yet another feature tested on N5 during that time was an internally installed wireless transmitting set to allow communication with the 'parent ship', powered by a folding wind-driven generator on the fuselage side just below the cockpit.

After an initial order for 50 Sopwith 2F1s, which began in the autumn of 1917, the Admiralty ordered a total of 650, though it later reduced that by almost half. William Beardmore & Co Ltd, which had previously built the Pup-inspired WB III shipboard fighter for the Navy, was the other main contractor, delivering its first 2F1, N6750, on 20 February 1918.

Appearing in 1918, Sopwith Monoplane No 2, aka the Swallow, had a parasol wing with a 6-degree sweepback, but the RAF report of its test programme in May 1919 revealed its performance to be inferior to that of the Camel biplane. (Jack Herris)

While the 'Ships Camels' were being built the British had been further reconfiguring HMS *Furious*. Having already lost one of its 18-inch gun turrets to make room for the forward flight deck, it had the aft turret removed and 300 more feet of decking built up over an aeroplane hangar, theoretically to ease on-board landings. In practice, such efforts remained difficult because the bridge and smokestack were still amidships. Nevertheless, the Royal Navy's first true aircraft carrier returned to sea on 15 March 1918 to carry a complement of 2F1s on anti-airship patrols in the North Sea.

Camels participated in a series of experiments with hydrovanes and ditching gear on the Isle of Grain in the summer of 1918. On 9 August Camel B3878 was ditched with a nine-inch steel hydrovane in the front axle and a negative hydrovane on a long stail skid. It alit smoothly into the water but then tipped on its nose and began to sink. In September the station reported ditching a Camel with a wooden hydrovane and smaller wheels into a 15 mph wind, resulting in its planning smoothly and then sinking gently without nosing up. Two subsequent attempts involved the same procedure with the addition of jettisoning the wheels – when the pilot withdrew pins from the axle, powerful springs shot the wheels off. These landings were reported 'entirely successful so that the fear is now considered satisfactory'.

The naval air station at Felixstowe saw some interesting experiments with Ships Camels. Lt Stuart Douglas Culley and a warrant shipwright at Felixstowe devised a jettisonable undercarriage for the fighter to aid ditching at sea, which Lt R. E. Keys, DFC successfully demonstrated on 20 September 1918. From July 1918 on, experiments were conducted with a 'little crook anchoring gear' that suspended an aeroplane beneath the obsolescent airship *R23*, from which the 'parasite fighter' could be launched. After a three-hour flight on 3 October, the experiment reached its climax on 6 November when Lt Keys, with the engine of Camel N6814 idling at 500rpm, rode under *R23* to an altitude of 3,000 feet, at which point the 2F1 was released. After a 10-foot drop he got into a stable glide, revved up the engine and flew on to a successful landing.

As of 31 October 1918 129 2F1 Camels were in the RAF inventory, all but 17 serving in the Grand Fleet. Further production by Fairey, Pegler and Sage were cancelled with the armistice. As it was, Ships Camels served aboard four aircraft carriers, 10 battleships and 17 cruisers in the course of the type's career, during which it made its own share of history.

A Sopwith 2F1 'Ships Camel', powered by a 150-hp AR 1 rotary engine developed by W. O. Bentley (later redesignated BR 1), shows the metal cabane strut and armament that distinguished it from its landlubber cousin. (Greg Van Wyngarden)

2Lt William S. Lockhart flies 2F1 Camel N6822 from a deck erected atop a gun turret aboard light cruiser HMAS *Sydney*. (Greg Van Wyngarden)

OPERATIONAL HISTORY

Western Front

On 11 July 1917, about two months after the Camel made its debut with the RNAS, No 70 Sqn became the first RFC unit equipped with the new fighter. For a time its veteran crews soldiered on in their 1½-Strutters while the pilots adapted to the Camel's radically livelier characteristics. On the 12th Capt Noel W. Webb, in B3756, assisted two 1½ Strutter crews in forcing Albatros C X 9289/16 of *Fl Abt* (*Lichtbild*) 18 to land at Bellevue aerodrome, where it flipped over on its back. The observer, Ltn Johannes Wollenhaupt, was taken prisoner but the pilot, Ltn d R. Johannes Böhm, died of his wounds the next day.

On 17 July Webb led a five-Camel patrol four miles into enemy territory, where they were jumped by about 30 Albatros D Vs of *Jasta* 6 and 8 south of Gheluvelt. Webb was credited with two D Vs out of control; 2Lt J. C. Smith claimed another in a vertical dive before breaking through the enemy formation, firing as he went, to regain Allied lines, while 2Lt E. Cribben saw smoke issue from the engine of one of his adversaries before he disengaged, guns jammed, and landed at La Lovie. Lts C. S. Workman, in Camel B3779, and W. E. Grosset, in B6332, were not so fortunate – the former was killed, probably by Ltn d R. Robert Tüxen of *Jasta* 6, while Grosset was brought down by Vzfw Rudolf Franke of *Jasta* 8 and captured. Neither German unit recorded any casualties, but Ltn Karl Meyer of *Jasta* 11 was wounded, probably by Webb.

The discrepancy between credited successes and actual enemy losses in these encounters typified a large percentage of the claims that, accepted on face value by the British, gave the Camel its status as having the highest victory tally of any single fighter in World War I. Within such exaggerated scoring, however, the Camels occasionally took a genuine toll on the enemy, as was the case on the evening of 26 July, when a mixed bag of British fighters – SPADs of No 19 Sqn, SE 5s of 56 Sqn, Camels of 70 Sqn, Triplanes of Naval

8 and de Havilland DH 5s of 32 Sqn – battled some 30 Albatros scouts at three altitude levels over Gheluvelt. Lts Leonard Barlow and Gerald J. C. Maxwell of 56 were credited with two enemy 'driven down' for the loss of eight-victory Scottish ace and 'B' Flight leader Capt Phillip B. Prothero – killed by Vzfw Alfred Muth of *Jasta* 27, whose only casualty, Ltn Hans Helmigt, was recorded as 'injured in an accident'. Lt Smith of 70 Sqn was also credited with one 'driven down', but Webb claimed an Albatros that shed its wings – and whose death plunge was witnessed by others – which turned out to be Ltn Otto Brauneck, a nine-victory ace of *Jasta* 11. Webb had to land his own shot-up Camel B3756 in Allied lines, but he was unharmed and his probable assailant, Ltn Franz Götte of *Jasta* 20, was more strictly, but rightly, denied confirmation as an official victory.

Webb swiftly raised his total to 14 by 13 August, also receiving a Bar to the Military Cross he'd been awarded for the five previous victories he'd scored flying FE 2bs with No 25 Sqn. His luck ran out near Polygon Hill on 16 August, however, when he and B3756 fell victim to even more skilful foe – Ltn Werner Voss of *Jasta* 10.

On 31 July the British launched a new Flanders offensive that came to be called the Third Battle of Ypres or Passchendaele. That agonising 'push' was still grinding on when the Camel's most famous counterpart made its first appearance in the form of two Fokker F Is, pre-production precursors of the Dr I triplane, undergoing combat evaluation in *Jagdgeschwader* I. The *Geschwaderführer*, Rittm Manfred *Freiherr* von Richthofen, drew first blood in F I 102/17 with an RE 8 on 1 September and a Pup on the 3rd. On the latter date Werner Voss, possibly flying F I 103/17, downed a Camel north of Houthem, killing Lt A. T. Heywood of No 45 Sqn RFC.

At that point von Richthofen went on three weeks' leave, leaving Ltn Kurt von Döring in acting command of JG I and his triplane to Ltn Kurt Wolff, victor over 33 Allied aeroplanes, who was given command of *Jasta* 11 on 11 September.

Meanwhile, Voss had adapted his natural flying talents to F I 103/17, with which he brought down a Pup of 46 Sqn in Allied lines and destroyed a Caudron G6 of French *escadrille* C 53 on 5 September, followed the next day with an FE 2d of 20 Sqn. On the 10th Voss destroyed two 70 Sqn Camels, killing 2Lts A. J. S. Sisley and O. C. Pearson, followed 20 minutes later by a SPAD VII of Spa 37.

On the 11th Voss destroyed two more 45 Sqn Camels, his victims including six-victory ace Lt Oliver L. McMaking. Voss in turn was twice credited as driven down out of control to Capt Norman Macmillan, who believed there to be three triplanes in the fight – quite a comment on both the

Suspended beneath HMA R23 at Pulham Airship Base, 2F1 Camel N6814 awaits testing. It was successfully launched from the airship with Lt R. E. Keys of No 212 Sqn in the cockpit on 5 November 1918. (Greg Van Wyngarden)

A 2F1 Camel lands aboard HMS Argus *in late 1918. Although it entered service too late to see combat,* Argus *featured the first completely open flight deck, at last making landings as practicable as take-offs for its aircraft. (Colin A. Owers via Greg Van Wyngarden)*

aeroplane and its pilot. Voss was in fact untouched, with his overall tally now standing at 47.

The next clash of Camel and triplane would have a different outcome on the 15th, as Albatros D Vs of *Jasta* 11 attacked a four-aeroplane flight from Naval 10 over Mooselede and were joined by the recently promoted Obltn Wolff in F I 102/17. The Camels evaded the enemy's fire and in the dogfight that followed Flt Sub-Lt Norman M. Macgregor fired into the triplane at 25 yards' distance, saw it fall in a steep dive and was credited with an 'out of control' that proved to have substance: Wolff was subsequently found dead in the wreckage of his Fokker near Nachtigal.

The question of whether a Camel pilot could prevail against Voss and his triplane became moot on 23 September. After destroying a de Havilland DH 4 of No 57 Sqn that morning, Voss led five *Jasta* 10 fighters on an evening patrol, only to leave it to dive on a flight of SE 5as of No 60 Sqn. He was in turn attacked by two flights of No 56 Sqn SE 5as, resulting in an epic 10-minute fight in which Voss riddled several of his opponents before being shot down and killed by Lt Arthur P. F. Rhys Davids.

The short but spectacular career of the Fokker F Is put the seal of approval on the Fokker Dr I, but a rash of wing failures due to poor quality control led to their withdrawal in early November. The ultimate duel between Camel and triplane would have to wait until February 1918.

Meanwhile, a bit of Voss' fame rubbed off on a Camel pilot a month after his death. On 22 September Capt Thomas Frederic Williams of No 45 Sqn survived being shot down during a run-in with the Richthofen Circus, probably credited to Ltn Kurt Wüsthoff of *Jasta* 4. Then, on 24 October – 12 days after celebrating his 32nd birthday – the spry Camelier from Woodstock, Ontario, found himself isolated in the midst of seven Albatros D Vs, but used his Camel's agility to fend them off, reportedly sending their leader down to crash for his first victory. His squadron mates called him 'Voss' Williams thereafter, but he achieved one feat his namesake did not: he escaped to fight another day.

After again surviving being brought down on 6 November, this time in error by Canadian ground fire, Williams next scored a double – an Albatros in flames and another out of control – two days later. Serving on in Italy with 45 and 28 Sqns, he would eventually be credited with 13 victories, publish a volume of poetry at age 97 and die on 25 July 1985, less than three months short of his 100th birthday.

A new role was thrust upon the Camel when the Germans began making systematic and often devastating use of their two-seaters for ground attack in late September, including a smaller, more compact and nimble specialist, the Halberstadt CL II. The RFC responded by using DH 5s, which had proven disappointing as fighters but reasonably reliable and rugged at low altitudes – in the ground attack role. At the same time racks for up to four 20 or 25lb Cooper bombs were installed behind the undercarriage of the Camels and they too were pressed into service as trench strafers. The pilots were far from enthused about such 'dirty work', but in compensation for its lack of armour protection the erratic manoeuvres at which the Camel was capable served to make it an elusive target to enemy gunners.

A typical combination of fighter and ground attack roles came into play when Nos 28 and 70 Sqns raided an airfield whose residents included the crack *Jasta* Boelcke. One of 70 Sqn's flight leaders, Cedric N. Jones, described the mission:

'On 20th October 1917 four Camels from the Squadron, each carrying two 25lb bombs, with eight Camels as escort, together with a patrol of Spads from 23 Sqn as high offensive escort, attacked the German aerodrome at Rumbeke. The bombing attack was carried out from 400 feet; some of the bombs fell on Albatros D.Vs lined up on the airfield, blowing one to pieces; another burst just inside a hangar, and the remainder fell on hangars and sheds.

'The Camels, having released their bombs, then flew across the aerodrome firing at German ground personnel and into hangars and buildings. This machine gun attack was carried out at a height of 20 feet, and the undercarriage of [Lt Frank H.] Hobson's Camel was certainly run along the ground during the low attack as his wheels were widely splayed out when he landed.

'The escort was quite low at 2,000 feet and was led by Captain [Frederic] Laurence, "B" Flight, and myself, "A" Flight.

'Unluckily the Spads of 23 Squadron were involved in a fight on the way out to Rumbeke and thus were not with us on the return journey, which was unfortunate when we were heavily attacked by large numbers of Albatros scouts. The Huns appeared out the east wind haze and I mistook them at first for the Spads which were somewhat Hunnish in appearance. I found out my mistake when I saw them firing smoke tracer, and "A" and "B" Flights started circling to meet the attack.

'I think it must have been at this time that I lost Lieutenant Wilson, my deputy leader, because he did not return. My Camel was badly shot up during the attack and in the scrap that followed, and one of my gun cables was cut and the aluminium carburettor air intake was perforated by a bullet.'

In the melee with *Jasta* Boelcke's pilots 2Lt Alfred Koch fired 20 close-range rounds to drive an Albatros D V down out of control, then fired 80 rounds at another which force landed on the field. Coming under attack by three more D Vs, he then dropped to 300 feet and hedgehopped home. Two-seaters were sent crashing on or near the aerodrome by 2Lt J. Michie, 2Lt Edward B.

One of two Camel pilots credited with six enemy planes in one day, 19-year-old Lt John Lightfoot Trollope of No 43 Squadron scored the last three of his 18 victories – a balloon and two Albatros D Vs – on 28 March 1918, but was then brought down PoW by Ltn Paul Billik of *Jasta* 52, with wounds that necessitated the amputation of his left hand. (Jon Guttman)

Britain's only other 'sextuple ace', Capt Henry W. Woollett, also from 43 Sqn, got his six on 12 April 1918 in Boulton & Paul-built Camel D6402 – along with six more planes and 11 balloon of his 35 victory total. In March 1918 he experimented with a blotchy camouflage scheme to help in his anti-balloon attacks, but was quickly ordered to remove it. (Les Rogers via Aaron Weaver)

Booth, Lt Francis G. Quigley and Lt C. W. Primeau. On his return flight Primeau shot up another aerodrome, and he and Hobson strafed a train on the Menin-Roulers railway from 50 feet altitude.

In all the 70 Sqn Camel pilots claimed four enemy aeroplanes for the loss of Lt J. R. Wilson, killed, and 2Lt F. B. Farquharson, PoW. *Jasta* Boelcke credited those Camels to Ltn d R. Friedrich Kempf and Ltn Gerhard Bassenge, respectively, for the loss of Ltn d R. Walter Lange, killed near Becelaere.

Nearby, 28 Sqn scrapped with *Jasta* 35, resulting in victories credited to Capt William G. Barker, Lt James H. Mitchell and 2Lt P. G. Mulholland. *Jasta* 35's only recorded casualty was Uffz Emil Barnheine, wounded north-west of Roulers, while Ltn Ludwig Hanstein was credited with a Camel south-west of Moorslede. His victim, Sikh pilot 2Lt Hardit Singh Malik, reached Allied lines before force landing and flipping Camel B3887 over on its back. Malik emerged unhurt and his aeroplane was repaired and back in service with 45 Sqn in Italy by January 1918.

Prior to his flying exploits with 28 Sqn, Malik had broken through a wall of English prejudice to get into the RFC, but there was a second Indian pilot flying Camels in the autumn of 1917. On 14 September, however, 2Lt Errol Suva Chandra Sen's fighting career with 70 Sqn was abruptly curtailed as he was brought down in Camel B2333 by Vzfw Gustav Schneidewind of *Jasta* 17, to spend the rest of the war in Holzminden prison. On 26 October Malik was wounded in the leg, after a long, wild chase, by Ltn Paul Strähle of *Jasta* 18, but he made Allied lines before coming down and Strähle's claim was not confirmed. Malik subsequently flew Bristol F 2B Fighters with No 141 (HD) Sqn at Biggin Hill and with 11 Sqn RAF at Nivelles.

The launching of the last German bid for victory on the Western Front, '*der Kaiserschlacht*', on 21 March 1918, would see the classic clash between Camel and Fokker Dr I that enshrined both tight-turning dogfighters in World War I lore, with little to choose between them. 'Not even the Fokker triplane could follow a Camel in a right-handed bank', stated Capt Henry Winslow Woollett of No 43 Sqn, whose 35 victories included six in one day on 6 April – but, interestingly, not one triplane. In interesting counterpoint, Fokker Dr I pilots were advised to escape a Camel with a right-hand turn, supposedly the Camel's forte, implying that the triplane's turning circle was even tighter!

Believed to be B7184, brought down on 23 January 1918, this captured Camel was flown in *Jasta* 23b markings by its CO, Ltn Otto Kissenberth, in preference to the Roland D VIbs that equipped his unit. He used it to shoot down an SE 5a on 16 May, but while taking off on the 29th, the engine stopped and the ensuing crash from 40 metres altitude caused injuries that put Kissenberth out of the war. (Andy Kemp)

Besides Woollett, another Camel pilot of No 43 Sqn was credited with six victories: Capt John L. Trollope, on 24 March 1918. On the 28th he burned a balloon and downed two Albatros D Vs, bringing his total to 18 – again, none of them Fokker Dr Is – but was then brought down wounded by Ltn Paul Billik of *Jasta* 52, becoming a PoW and having to have his left hand amputated.

Rittm Manfred von Richthofen, the 'Red Baron', shot down eight Camels while flying the Dr I, including three aces – Capt Thomas S. Sharpe of No 73 Sqn, who had scored six victories in the two weeks prior to being brought down wounded as a PoW on 27 March; Capt Sydney P. Smith of 46 Sqn, with five victories when killed on 6 April; and Maj Richard Raymond-Barker, commander of No 3 Sqn with seven previous victories in Bristol Fighters, killed on 20 April. The long-standing claim that Capt A. Roy Brown of No 209 Sqn killed the German ace of aces the next day as he was pursuing Brown's friend 2Lt Wilfred R. May has since been dismissed in light of evidence making his demise at the hands of Australian ground fire far more likely. Even so, the exasperating refusal of the desperate May and his wildly jinking Camel to fall to his guns certainly played a part in von Richthofen's violating much of his own dicta, chasing the Canadian deep into Allied lines at low altitude in his fatally over-focused determination to bring him down. A later clash between 209 Sqn and the late Red Baron's 'Flying Circus' on 2 May had a clearer outcome: Ltn Hans Weiss, commander of *Jasta* 11 and a 16-victory ace, was killed by Lt Merill Samuel Taylor, his fifth of seven victories.

The Camel-triplane confrontations during the *Kaiserschlacht* were as short-lived as they were legendary. Mid-March 1918 had seen Camel strength on the Western Front reach 336 in 15 squadrons, while Dr I strength peaked at 171 in April. The arrival of the inline-engine Fokker D VII biplane in late May swiftly eclipsed its three-winged forebear, especially as the summer heat caused the ersatz castor oil used to lubricate the Dr I's rotary engines to break down and the engines to seize up.

Although the D VII was no match for the Camel in a turning dogfight, its savvier pilots tended to avoid such combats, much as American fighter pilots in World War II learned to avoid dogfighting the Mitsubishi A6M2 Zero, preferring to dive, zoom, turn and either re-engage head-on or seek the opportunity to latch onto one's tail. The Camel's stablemate, the SE 5a, was far better suited to matching the D VII at such tactics, but both British types soldiered on gamely until the last months of the war, when the first Sopwith Snipes began to replace Camels in No 43 Sqn RAF and No 4 Sqn AFC.

On 20 June the 17th Aero Sqn, USAS, was declared operational with a complement of 110-hp Le Rhône engine Camels, followed in early July by the 148th Aero Sqn with Clerget-powered machines. Attached to the RAF's 65 Wing in Flanders, these American-flown Camels bore British cockades and, in contrast to the French-influenced Nieuport 28 and SPAD units fighting around Château Thierry at the time with colourful unit insignias, they were identified by abstract white symbols – a dumbbell and a triangle, respectfully, as well as individual letters and red, white or blue flight colours on the wheel hubs.

Most of the American Camel pilots had had previous experience attached to RAF squadrons, but more of them knew of it by reputation than from having actually flown one, and few were ready for the transition. One impression was recorded by the ever-outspoken 1Lt Elliott White Springs, who had scored four victories in SE 5as while attached to No 85 Sqn RAF before his reassignment to the 148th Aero Sqn at Petite-Synthe in July 1918:

'I went up there and found they were going to fly Sopwith Camels, a tricky little biplane with a 130 Clerget rotary motor and two Vickers guns firing through the prop. They would do about 90 level but you couldn't fly level because they would shake your teeth out in 40 seconds by the clock. You had to climb or glide. But they could fly upside down and turn inside a stairwell. They would stall at 15,000 feet and lose 1,000 feet in a turn. But they were deadly below 5,000 feet if you could suck the Fokkers down to that level.

'We picked up the cast-off rebuilt Camels from Aire. No new Camels had been built since January when they became obsolete and were replaced by SEs, Dolphins, Bentleys, and Snipes. But that summer they were still the workhorses below 15,000. A Camel was at a disadvantage at the beginning of a fight where speed and height were paramount, but in a dogfight down low nothing could get away from it. If the Fokkers didn't get them on their first dive they would often leave them alone and just pick at the stragglers. A Camel could make a monkey out of an SE or a Fokker at treetop level but it couldn't zoom and it couldn't dive. The Camel's guns were best at 100 yards. Beyond that you wasted bullets because of the terrific vibration.'

Another Yank from 85 Sqn was 1Lt Orville A. Ralston from Lincoln, Nebraska, who had two victories in SE 5as before he was notified of his transfer to the 148th on 4 September. The next day he wrote in his diary, 'I leave old 85 in a rather dejected mood and hate to be posted on Camels without instruction on Avros or Pups.'

Ralston arrived at Petite-Synthe on the 5th with a letter from 85 Sqn's CO, explaining: 'Lt. Ralston, USAS, who is posted to you, has done 140 hours over the lines on SEs. He has never flown a rotary engine of any kind, and I consider that if it is essential that he should fly Camels he should be given a period of training. To fly Camels without previous dual training I would think would be almost out of the question.'

A lineup of Camels of No 71 Sqn RFC – redesignated No 4 Sqn Australian Flying Corps – in March 1918. Sadly, with the general re-marking of fighter units amid the German Kaiserschlacht on 22 March the Aussies had to replace their boomerangs for a white bar ahead of the roundel. (Colin A. Owers)

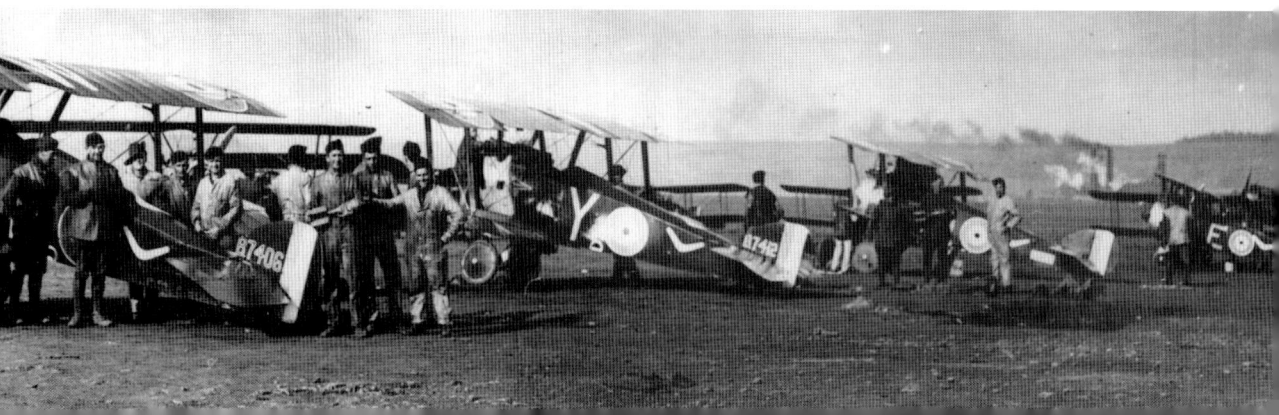

Capt Arthur H. Cobby's Camel E1416 of No 4 Sqn, Australian Flying Corps, undergoes maintenance at Serny in the summer of 1918. A former bank clerk from Melbourne, Cobby became the top-scoring AFC ace with 29 victories. His aluminium cut-out of Charlie Chaplin that he mounted on each of his Camels in turn is now preserved at the RAAF Point Cooke Museum. (Colin A. Owers)

On 6 September Ralston wrote: 'About 6:00 PM I decide to fly one and do take off but make an awful show. It makes me very nervous and I feel quite unsteady after flying the thing.'

He tried again the next morning and noted: 'The petrol and oil fumes make me very sick with headache. I make a bum landing and feel more inclined to be afraid of the machine. I want to try to make good here, for all of the fellows are real boys and I like the RAF system fine. I only hope I will feel better and can learn to fly this rotary engine without any accidents. It seems rather yellow to hold out any longer so in the evening I take up old Mr Camel and fly him okay.'

Although Ralston now had the aeroplane's measure, on the 12th he wrote: 'Our Camels are poor machines at best to cope with the late German Fokker, which is a marvel when handled correctly. So God spare our days until we move south and get stationary engines once more and in some "bus" that can keep pace with the Fokker when it comes to speed and climb.'

Forced to make the most of what he had, three days later Ralston teamed up with 1Lt Springs, Percy E. Cunnius and Henry C. Starkey to drive a Halberstadt two-seater down OOC over Epinoy. He went on to achieve acedom in the Camel with Fokker D VIIs destroyed on 26 September and 3 October.

An example of a 'natural pilot' was 1Lt George A. Vaughn Jr, an American SE 5a pilot with No 84 Sqn RAF who had seven victories when he was ordered on 29 August to take over 'B' Flight of the 17th Aero Sqn in the wake of its losses three days earlier. Although his only previous rotary engine experience had been on Pups – a better transition into the SE's cockpit than the Camel's – Vaughn, remarkably, got the feel for it shortly after take-off on his first operational patrol, and swiftly joined that lucky fraternity of 'Camel kings', writing: 'Although inherently unstable (rigged so tail-heavy that it would nose up and stall immediately if flown hands off), it was highly manoeuvrable, climbed well at low and medium altitudes and, when properly handled, was a most effective weapon for close-in air combat at those altitudes.'

Even though he did well in the Camel, adding six more to his tally, Vaughn still preferred the SE 5a, which besides being better at disengaging from

The highest scoring Camel pilot of all, Canadian Capt Donald Roderick MacLaren of No 46 Sqn neither smoke nor drank, carried half the prescribed ammunition to lighten his plane and scored 54 victories between 6 March and 9 October 1918, dying on 4 July 1989 at age 96. (National Aviation Museum, Ottawa, Ontario, Canada)

unfavourable odds – with the Camel, there was little recourse but to fight one's way out – he regarded the stable SE as a more comfortable aeroplane to fly. It was much more stable and less drafty inside the cockpit – with the added bonus of being able to warm his gloved hands during high altitude patrols by momentarily resting them over the hot ends of the exhaust pipes.

The Amiens offensive, which would put the initiative securely in the hands of British forces for the rest of the war, saw 19 Camel squadrons – Nos 3, 43, 45, 46, 54, 65, 73, 80, 151, 201, 203, 204, 208, 209, 210, 213, No 4 AFC, and 17th and 148th Aero Sqns, USAS – along the Western Front on 8 August. Serving alongside this Camel plurality were 12 SE 5a squadrons, six with Bristol F 2Bs and four with Sopwith Dolphins.

The early morning of the 8th saw the Camels bombing and strafing soldiers, supply dumps, gun emplacements and supply vehicles, flying at altitudes of between 50 and 100 feet at 30-minute intervals throughout the daylight hours. With 16,000 men taken prisoner, the remnants of the weary German 2. and 18. *Armees* retreated across the Somme River while, in an attempt to cut them off, Allied units tried to destroy the bridges and every German fighter unit in the vicinity, including elements of *Jagdgeschwader* I, II and III, converged to prevent that from happening. This precipitated one of the great air battles of the war, with the RAF claiming 276 German aeroplanes and balloons destroyed between 5 and 11 August, while losing 93 of its own aircraft.

The German fighter pilots included 25 Camels among the total of 139 RAF machines they claimed during that time period. Ground fire also took its toll, probably mortally wounding Capt Michael E. Gonne of 54 Sqn (5 victories) and Capt Eric G. Brookes of 65 Sqn (6) on 8 August, and Lt George D. Tod, a five-victory American ace in 65 Sqn, on the 9th.

Within the general British overclaiming, the Camels claimed one beyond dispute on 12 August, when Capt Robert M. Foster of 209 Sqn brought a Fokker D VII down intact in Allied lines, Offstv Fritz Blumenthal of *Jasta* 53 being taken PoW, for his 12th of 16 victories. On 13 August Capt Charles D. Booker, a former ace of Naval 8 now commanding 201 Sqn and victor over 29 opponents in Pups, Triplanes and Camels, was killed by Ltn Ulrich Neckel of *Jasta* 19. That evening, however, Capt Adrian J. B. Tonks and Lt H. W. M. Cumming of 204 Sqn sent a Fokker D VII down in a spin, the shared victory being credited as Tonks' seventh out of an eventual 12. His victim was most likely Ltn Dieter Collin, CO of *Jasta* 56 and 13-victory ace, who crash landed and died of his wounds in hospital soon after.

An example of what a Camel could do against Fokkers in the hands of a dextrous pilot occurred during a contact offensive patrol at 1700hrs by No 3 Sqn, in concert with SE 5as of 56 Sqn, when Fokker D VIIs of *Jasta* 26 were encountered. 'Had an interesting (???) time while it lasted', wrote Lt Robert McLeod in his diary. 'Was in lower formation, 8 Fokkers then attacked us, while 25 attacked the upper formations. Saw one SE go spinning down. 2 of our fellows got Fokkers out of control. One Fokker dived at me – I turned at him as he went past and fired a long burst at him. He was turning, and I didn't get him. 2 more got on my tail and I went down with engine on. As one dived

Le Rhône-powered Camel D9495 served with the 17th Aero Sqn, one of two US Army Air Service units attached to 65 Wing RAF during the autumn of 1918. The 17th scored some notable successes and suffered some painful losses, including six planes on 26 August 1918. (Les Rogers via Aaron Weaver)

at me, I turned in under him. Then the other son-of-a-gun came at me and I did a split dive under him, and so on down to 2,000 feet. I was near our lines, and they left. Only got a half-dozen bullet holes in the bus. Climbed back to find formation, but couldn't find it. Came back home and they arrived at same time. 2 hours.'

Jasta 26 suffered no casualties, while Ltn Claus Riemer, Vzfw Fritz Classen and Vzfw Christian Mesch claimed Camels and Ltn Marchard claimed an SE 5a. Only the latter two were credited, and 2Lt Noel F. Bishop of 56 Sqn was killed. It may very well be that McLeod's precipitate dive was misinterpreted by ground observers as well as his German attackers to make him Mesch's 'confirmed victim'.

Although they soldiered on to the end, the war's last months were not kind to the Camel squadrons, which sometimes suffered heartbreaking losses. On 26 August, first day of the British assault on the Scarpe, JG III's seasoned Fokker D VII pilots killed 1Lt George V. Siebold of the 148th Aero Sqn and five members of the 17th Aero Sqn, as well as bringing down the latter's 1Lt William D. Tipton as a PoW. No 43 Sqn lost four men as PoWs and one killed on the 29th, mostly at the hands of Paul Strähle's *Jasta* 57, which paid with one Fokker brought down in flames in which Vzfw Knobel was wounded but survived.

An encounter with *Jasta* Boelcke on 2 September resulted in the 148th Aero Sqn losing two men killed and two as PoWs, while 1Lt Field Kindley nursed his damaged Camel into Allied lines. No 70 Sqn lost a staggering eight Camels with four men killed and four as PoWs on the 4th. In a sprawling battle with *Marine Feld Jasta* II and IV on 14 October, 213 Sqn lost six pilots, all killed, while MFJ IV lost Ltn z S. Max Stinsky. On the 23rd No 204 Sqn (the former Naval 4, which had given the Camel its combat debut) fought MFJ I and II, killing the latter's Ltn z S. Hermann Bargmann, but losing five of its own pilots, all killed. Four days later 204 Sqn lost another four aeroplanes – three men killed, one PoW – adding further to its dubious status as the Camel unit with the highest overall casualties.

Even as late as 4 November the *Luftstreitkräfte* was full of fight, *Jasta* 29 accounting for four Camels of No 65 Sqn for the loss of Uffz Paul Schönfelder, in spite of 65 Sqn's claim of eight enemy destroyed, six out of control and another driven down. Elsewhere, FlgMstr Gerhard Hubrich of MFJ IV downed two more 204 Sqn Camels, killing one pilot while the other force landed unharmed in Allied lines; the British claimed two enemy destroyed and

Clerget-powered Camel F1400 of the 148th Aero Sqn, based at Petite-Synthe aerodrome, sported an airscrew spinner decorated with a skull and crossbones, and was regularly flown by 1Lt Errol H. Zistel. Continuing his flying career post-war, 'Zip' Zistel retired in 1957 as a major general in the Ohio Air National Guard. (Les Rogers via Aaron Weaver)

five out of control, but MFJ IV recorded no losses. It may be noted that on that same day *Jasta* Boelcke claimed five of the Camel's successors, Snipes of No 4 Sqn AFC – four of them by the CO, Obltn Karl Bolle – for the loss of Uffz Otto Hägele, killed.

The last Camel claims of the war were made on 10 November: a DFW credited to Capt William Jenkins of 210 Sqn, followed by an LVG crashed by a flight of 213 Sqn Camels led by Capt George C. MacKay, and finally a Fokker D VII driven down by Jenkins for his 12th victory. Their last fatalities were Lt J. E. Pugh of 210 Sqn, possibly an 'SE 5' credited to Lt d R. Hans Holthusen of *Jasta* 29, and 2Lts G. E. Dowler and W. G. Coulthurst of 46 Sqn, who were just taking off when their aeroplanes collided and crashed to earth in flames.

The most successful of all the Camel pilots was Donald Roderick MacLaren of No 46 Sqn, described by squadronmate Arthur Gould Lee as 'the non-smoking, non-drinking Canadian from Vancouver, who after three quiet months to learn the trade became the squadron's top ace, obtaining 54 victories in six months.' Arriving in France on 23 November 1917, MacLaren flew Pups until 150-hp Le Rhône powered Camels replaced them in late January 1918. 'They were able to cope with Albatros, Fokker D VII and Fokker Tripes', MacLaren declared. 'They lacked speed but were more turnable than the later Sopwith Snipe.'

Perhaps more of a factor than piloting skill was MacLaren's marksmanship and his penchant, after an early experience with jammed guns, for personally inspecting his weapons and interrupter gear before every mission. 'I perhaps did more flying on my own between patrols', he added, 'and carried less ammunition – not over 600 rounds – to reduce weight.' Not only was he credited with 54 victories between March and October 1918, but after a distinguished career in Canadian civil aviation he lived to be 96, dying on 4 July 1989.

The armistice found Camels serving in 18 squadrons on the Western Front, but their days were clearly numbered – No 208 Sqn was re-equipping with Snipes and 80 Sqn would be fully re-equipped in December. For a few months they served on with Allied occupation forces, but by March 1919 most units had been reduced to cadre strength. At least 50 Camels were bequeathed to the Belgians, who had flown them in combat alongside the more popular Hanriot HD 1. The last Camels were retired from RAF service by January 1920.

Italy

On 25 October 1917 the Austro-Hungarians, bolstered by German ground and air forces (the latter of which including *Jastas* 1, 31 and 39), routed the Italian army at Caporetto and drove it back 70 miles to the Piave River. In response Britain and France sent contingents of their own in November, the RFC's contribution including Nos. 34 and 42 squadrons, equipped with RE 8s, and Camel-equipped Nos 28, 45 and 66 Sqns.

Settling in at Grossa on 28 November, 28 Sqn drew first blood the next day when its aggressive Canadian 'C' Flight leader, Capt Bill Barker, claimed an Albatros that shed its wings. On 3 December he shot an Albatros down in flames and then burned a kite balloon, strafing the winch crew and driving an enemy staff car into a ditch for good measure. The German Albatros pilot, Ltn Franz von Kerssenbrock of *Jasta* 39, was killed, as was the Austrian balloon observer, Ltn M. Riegert of *Ballon Kompagnie* 10.

Disappointed in the relative inactivity over the Italian front, Barker elected to stir something up on 25 December, when he and Lt Harold Byron Hudson flew 10 miles into enemy territory to Motta di Livensa aerodrome, where they dropped a large piece of cardboard inscribed: 'To the Austrian Flying Corps from the English R.F.C., wishing you a very Merry Christmas'. The two then proceeded to shoot up the airfield, setting fire to a hangar and damaging four aircraft.

Although the Canadians' holiday message was meant for the Austro-Hungarians, the recipient was *Fl Abt (A)* 204, and its German personnel were not amused. Next day *Fl Abt* 2 launched a retaliatory bombing raid on Trevignano field, whose occupants were all Italian. This stirred up a fresh hornet's nest, in the form of 16 Hanriot HD 1s of the 70*a*, 76*a*, 78*a* and 82*a Squadriglie*. Although the unescorted DFW C Vs dropped one bomb on a

Clayton & Shuttleworth-built Camel D3336 flies on patrol with No 210 Sqn. Lt Kenneth R. Ungar, a volunteer from Newark, New Jersey, who had joined the RAF after being turned down by the USAS, destroyed a Fokker D VII while flying this machine on 28 September 1918 for his ninth of 14 victories. (Michael O'Neal)

Commandant Robert Dhanis, Belgium's 35th licensed aviator, carried out 200 wartime missions from 1914 and flew this Camel, bearing the holly leaf emblem of his 3ème *Escadrille*, as an escort to the unit's normal complement of Breguet 14A2s. (Van der Merckt via Walter Pieters)

hangar of the 76a *Squadriglia*, wrecking or damaging a few HD 1s, killing six ground personnel and injuring some others, the Italians and some 28 Sqn Camel pilots pounced on them and claimed eight of the two-seaters.

A second wave of Germans included the first AEG G.IV twin-engine bombers to appear over Italy, courtesy of *Kasta* 19, *Kampfgeschwader* 4. Two more DFWs and one of the AEGs was shot down this time, the latter having run a gauntlet that resulted in it being credited to Capt James Mitchell of 28 Squadron, *Sottotenente* Silvio Scaroni of the 76a and *Sergente* Giacomo Brenta of the 78a *Squadriglia*. The Germans claimed three enemy fighters in the course of the raids, but neither the Italians nor the British had lost anything.

Another run-in with the Germans occurred on 11 January 1918, when an RE 8 of No 42 Sqn and its six Camel escorts from 45 Sqn came under attack by 10 Albatros scouts: a *Kette* each from *Jasta* 1 and 39. In spite of the odds, the Camel pilots strove to keep one of their number near their two-seat charge. Two Albatros out of control were claimed by 2Lt Earl McNabb Hand, both subsequently disallowed, before he disengaged with half his tailplane shot away, a gun cowling holed and his centre section riddled. In spite of that damage he force landed unhurt at Villorba. His Camel, B2430, was eventually repaired and returned to service.

Capt 'Voss' Williams stuck by the RE 8 in spite of three attempts by one German to get on his tail, each time waiting until his opponent dived close before executing a sharp turn to engage and foil the attack. He was credited with one Albatros out of control. The last Williams saw of his wingman, 2Lt D. W. Ross, he had rocked his wings to signal that the enemy was coming down, while he gestured back to close up because he was too high. He lost track of Ross in the ensuing melee, and his fate remained unknown until several weeks later, when a German aeroplane dropped a message to the British that he had been buried with military honours at San Fior di Sopra.

In a three-minute duel with an Albatros Lt H. T. Thompson, an Australian from New South Wales, was struck near his throat, but then managed to swing behind it and drove it down in a dive, only to find two more enemies on his tail. Making a right-hand climbing turn, he got behind one antagonist, fired a burst at 20 feet and saw the Albatros dive into the ground near Vittorio. Five or six more Germans then got on his tail and, out of ammunition, he fled. A bullet struck his thumb and smashed the revolution counter in front of his face. Another struck his propeller, causing the engine to vibrate. Thompson pulled back on the throttle and all the Germans overshot him. When he reached the Adriatic Sea, they headed home.

After climbing to 8,000 feet and flying to a river mouth (the Po, it turned out), Thompson turned inland and, when his petrol ran out, landed in a farm field near Mirandilla. There, his wounds were tended by Italian civilians, who made him an honoured guest and later christened the nearby farmhouse 'Tomsonia Aeroplani'. Both he and his repaired Camel, B2494, rejoined the squadron.

Belgium acquired at least 50 Camels, some of which served in the 9ème Escadrille – whose pilots preferred Hanriot HD 1s – and principally in the 11ème Escadrille as shown here. *Adj* Léon Cremers, who claimed a German two-seater on 31 October 1918 that was not confirmed, liked to take his violin on patrols, until it fell out of the plane during a loop. He was killed in a post-war Hanriot crash on 7 June 1919. (Van der Merckt via Walter Pieters)

Both Hand's and Ross' experiences show how the Camel's durability as much as its agility could save the life of a good pilot, as well as take the life of a careless one. Hand and the less fortunate Ross were credited to Obltn Josef Loeser and Vzfw Wilhelm Hippert of *Jasta* 39. The second Albatros that Thompson saw crash was probably Obltn Hans Kummetz, CO of *Jasta* 1 and a seven-victory ace, who was killed at Conegliano.

The German units were withdrawn from Italy in the spring of 1918 to take part in the last great offensive on the Western Front, leaving the Allied air arms to deal solely with the Austro-Hungarian *Fliegerkompagnien*, or *Fliks*. The Camel pilots often found their airmen to be as worthy foes as their German Allies had been. Even so, it seems likely that an Albatros claimed over Motta di Livensa by Capt Mitchell of No 28 Sqn on 4 February was flown by Hptm Godwin Brumowski, commander of *Flik* 41/J and Austria's ace of aces. In a letter to Obltn Frank Linke-Crawford, Brumowski said he was leading Stabsfeldwebel Karoly Kaszala and Zugsführer Alfred Brand on patrol when he was attacked by 'wretched English' over Passarella, between Piave and Piave-Vecchia, stating: 'Alone against eight because my other gentlemen had no desire for the attack, I received 26 hits. Gasoline, bracing wires, motor *kaputt*.' Although the lower wing of his Oeffag-built Albatros D III 153.52 was also shredded, and the fighter turned over during his forced landing, Brumowski survived the experience, and ultimately the war with 35 victories to his name.

Among the members of No 66 Sqn at San Pietro in Gu in March 1918 are, standing, second from left, Lt Christopher McEvoy (9 victories); twelfth, 2Lt Gordon F. Mason Apps (10); and thirteenth, 2Lt Gerald A. Birks (12). Those seated include, third from left, 2Lt Stanley Stanger (13 victories), fifth, Maj John T. P. Whittaker, squadron CO; seventh, 2Lt Alan Jerrard, VC (7); eighth, Capt Peter Carpenter (24); and Lt Harold R. Eycott-Martin (8). (G. A. Birks Album via Jon Guttman)

Flown by Capt James Hart Mitchell, Camel B6344 of No 28 Sqn bore the flight leader's number '1' in France, but replaced it with a more standard RFC-style individual letter 'G' after the move to Italy. Mitchell scored six of his 11 victories in this plane, his victim of 4 February 1918 possibly being Austrian ace of aces Godwin Brumowski. (Les Rogers via Aaron Weaver)

On that same day five Camels from 45 Sqn were patrolling at 12,000 feet near Sernaglia when they came upon eight Albatros D Vs about to pounce on two reconnoitring RE 8s. Being 2,000 feet above the Camels, the Albatros dived on them instead, but failed to score a hit before overshooting. The next thing they knew, the Camels were above and behind them. The Scottish flight leader, Capt Matthew B. Frew, sent the enemy leader, described as having a red nose and black and white chequered fuselage, down to crash near Barbisano Collato, while Lt H. D. O'Neill downed another at Marcatello, Lt Alfred J. Haines sent one crashing at Susegana for his first of an eventual six victories, and 'Bunty' Frew drove two off the tail of Canadian Lt D. G. McLean, seeing one go down OOC for his 23rd and final victory before being shipped home. McLean, who was just 13 days with the squadron, also drove one down to crash, but on the way back to base his Camel, B2494, was fatally struck by an anti-aircraft artillery shell. The Camels' opponents on this occasion were again from German *Jasta* 39, the CO, Obltn Loeser, and Uffz Dierenfeld both being credited with Camels before coming down wounded near Barbisano, while Vzfw Rudolf Wiesner was killed.

Mitchell and B6344 were a bit less fortunate on 18 March, when he was dived upon by five Albatros 20 miles behind enemy lines. Turning up underneath the first aeroplane, he fired about 60 rounds into it at 20 yards distance and saw it go down in flames. He was engaging a second Albatros when a third and fourth hit him in the engine and fuel tank. Fleeing with four

E CAMELS OVER MONTE TOMBA

On 2 May 1918 newly formed *Fliegerkompagnie* 68/J encountered Camels of No 66 Sqn over Monte Tomba, resulting in 2Lts Frederick N. Marchant, Norman S. Taylor and Gerald A. Birks each claiming an Albatros, while Capt Charles M. Maud claimed an 'LVG' two-seater. In actuality, Oeffag Albatros D III 153.176 force landed with its engine dead and its pilot, Ltn d R Kajetan Kosinski, wounded, probably by Birks. When *Flik* 68/J again ran into 66 Sqn Camels over Vidor on 4 May, two Albatros were credited to Birks, two to 2Lt Gordon F M Apps, one to Lt Vivian S Parker and one to Lt William C. Hilborn. Again the truth fell short of the RAF claims, but was bad enough for the Austro-Hungarians, who lost their commander, five-victory ace Oblt Karl Patzelt, in 153.182, and Flugzeugsführer Franz Fritsch in 153.210. Stabsfeldwebel Andreas Dombrowski, in Oeffag Albatros D III 153.195, was credited with a Camel in flames for his sixth victory before being forced to land near Piave de Soligo and miraculously survived a strafing by 2Lt George D. McLeod of 28 Sqn (also credited with an Albatros) with his face grazed by a bullet. Montreal native Birks described the fate of his victims in a letter to the author: 'Both machines landed on our side of the front line (the only two that did). Franz Fritsch was the only name that I know of. I was very sorry for him. I shot his machine out of control at about 14,000 feet. All the way down he knew that he had to crash. Italian soldiers on the scene of his crash told me that his plane burst into flames at about 1,000 feet, and that he climbed out on a wing. They told me that he had jumped from about 300 feet, missing a large haystack by about a yard. They said that he lived for two or three hours. I have never met such a fine-looking or handsome young man. Patzelt was more fortunate. Ten seconds after I opened fire on him, he was burned to a crisp'.

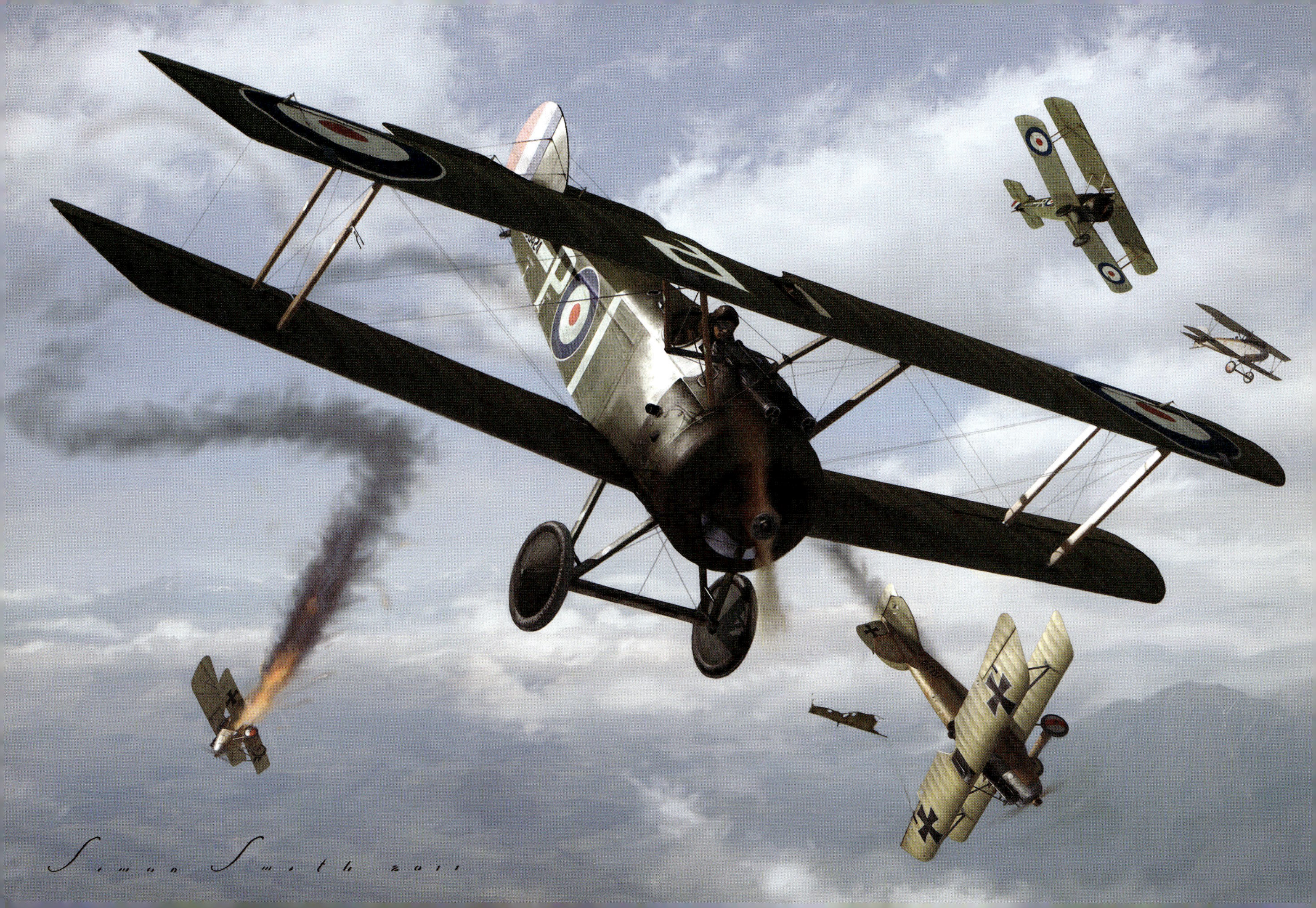
Simon Smith 2011

enemies on his tail, he managed to reach the Piave River, at which point, possibly under Italian anti-aircraft fire, they broke off, and Mitchell, unable to reach his own airfield at Grossa, force landed at Istrana. Austro-Hungarian records do not mention any losses in flames, but jointly credited a Camel to Feldwebel István Fejes and Korporal Franz Schwarzmann of Austro-Hungarian *Flik* 51/J. Notwithstanding their perception of his fate, Mitchell was back in B6344's cockpit to claim another Albatros D III in flames on 17 April.

No 66 Sqn made history of a sort on 30 March when three Camels led by Capt Peter Carpenter left their aerodrome at Pan Pietro in Gu, and at 1135hrs he spotted a 'Rumpler' two-seater escorted by four Albatros D IIIs returning to Austro-Hungarian territory at 1,400 feet altitude. By the time Carpenter led his Camels into a good attacking position with the sun at their backs, however, the two-seater was landing at Mansue, aerodrome of *Flik* 34/D.

Carpenter's flight then dived on the enemy scouts, at which point the British combat reports become confused and sometimes contradictory. Carpenter was credited with an Albatros, Lt Harold R. Eycott-Martin with two and 2Lt Alan Jerrard with three, in the process of which he also descended at least twice to attack Mansue aerodrome.

After all that the report stated that Jerrard rejoined his flight 'flying very weakly as though wounded', only to be followed by ten more Albatros. Jerrard allegedly turned and attacked them repeatedly until finally shot down, crashing four miles west of Mansue.

The combat report, apparently compiled from comments or jotted down statements by Carpenter and Eycott-Martin, done while still in a state of post-combat stress, was never signed by either pilot, only by squadron CO, Maj John T. P. Whittaker and/or the recording officer, Tech Capt William Topham, before going up the chain of command. Based on it, Jerrard was gazetted for the Victoria Cross on 1 May.

While 66 Sqn was compiling that stirring account of his extraordinary exploits, Alan Jerrard was sitting disconsolately beside the wreck of his Camel, B5648, until he met the man who shot him down, Oblt Benno Fiala, *Ritter* von Fernbrugg.

The report filed at Fiala's unit, *Flik* 51/J, told a rather different story from 66 Sqn's. Fiala, leading a four-aeroplane escort in Albatros D III 153.155, had just seen its two-seater charge land at Mansue and was turning for his own airbase at Ghirano when three Camels dived out of the sun. One attacked Fiala, but was driven off his tail by Feldwebel István Fejes in 153.142, and then engaged the Hungarian ace in a difficult combat before being seen descending in Italian lines, to be credited as Fejes' 11th victory. Fiala, joined by Zugsführer Eugen Bönsch in 153.140, pursued another Camel, fired 100 rounds into it and saw it force land at Gordo al Monticano, where it struck a tree, tearing off its left wing and twisting its rear fuselage. Upon landing at Ghirano, Fiala drove a car four kilometres to take charge of Jerrard and drive him to the army headquarters at Oderzo.

Although the Camels clearly did not destroy six out of up to 19 opponents, Jerrard had by all accounts given a spirited account of himself, as evidenced

The forlorn remains of 2Lt Alan Jerrard's Camel B5648 'E' near Gorgo del Molino after being shot down by Oblt Benno Fiala *Ritter* von Fernbrugg of Flik 51J on 30 March 1918, in an action that led to Jerrard becoming the only Camel pilot awarded the Victoria Cross. (Les Rogers via Aaron Weaver)

by the Austro-Hungarian record of three of the four aeroplanes being sent to *Fliegenstappenpark* for repairs. Fejes, who had been lightly wounded in the heel, counted 46 bullet holes in his aeroplane.

Born in Lewisham, London, on 3 December 1897, Jerrard had been educated at Oundle and Birmingham University before being commissioned a second lieutenant in the South Staffordshire Regiment on 2 January 1916. On 23 September he transferred into the RFC and after qualifying at the Central Flying School at Upavon with an above average assessment on 14 June 1917 he was posted briefly to No 20 Sqn before switching to a fighter assignment at SPAD VII equipped 19 Sqn. Surviving a crash on 5 August, upon recovery Jerrard took a refresher course in rotary engine aircraft and then arrived at 66 Sqn in Italy on 22 February 1918. He was credited with four victories before his reported 'hat trick' of 30 March.

On 18 November, following the surrender and breakup of the Hapsburg Empire, Jerrard escaped from prison and made his way back to England. There he was apparently astonished to learn that his presence was requested at Buckingham Palace on 5 April 1919, when King George V awarded him the VC. He also received the Italian *Medaglia di Bronzo al Valore Militare*.

Returning to service, Jerrard served with the British detachment at Murmansk during the Russian Civil War in 1919. He retired from the RAF due to ill health in 1933, and died on 14 May 1968.

On 15 June the Austro-Hungarians launched their last attempt at a decisive breakthrough, simultaneously attacking the Italians along the Piave, the French on Monte Grappa and the British on the Asiago Plateau. Over the next three days the three Camel squadrons were primarily engaged in bombing the bridges over the Piave and strafing the ground troops. Heavy rains accomplished more, however, propelling tree trunks with the torrent to batter and sweep away the bridges one by one, until only two, near Santa Dona di Piave, remained usable by the afternoon of 18 June. Austro-Hungarian troops who had advanced to Montello found themselves cut off and isolated. The next day saw the Italians counterattack, while the Camels were authorised to resume sweeping the skies of enemy aeroplanes.

Although the Camels added significantly to their laurels throughout the Italian campaign, the RAF's relatively lax confirmation procedures, combined with the tendency to confuse the Camel with Italy's Macchi-built Hanriot HD 1, was sometimes the cause of resentment and friction between the British and their allies. Italian ace of aces Francesco Baracca expressed it in a letter home on 27 April: 'British airmen are apparently shooting down enemy aeroplanes

Newly arrived and yet to be assembled, Sopwith-built Camel B6424 was flown by 2Lt Gerald A. Birks of No 66 Sqn (standing before it) to score five victories from March to May 1918, including Austro-Hungarian aces Karl Patzelt (5 victories) and Jozsef Kiss (19). (G. A. Birks album via Jon Guttman)

with the greatest of ease, although we are able to verify that their opponents, rather than crashing, manage to fly away healthier than before.'

British overclaiming notwithstanding, not all the Camel pilots were worthy of Baracca's wry dismissal. Barker was loath to make unsubstantiated claims and a healthy percentage of his victories are borne out by enemy casualty records. More remarkably, 11 of the 12 victories credited to Montreal-born 2Lt Gerald A. Birks can be traced to known Austro-Hungarian losses – including the deaths of five-victory ace Obltn Karl Patzelt on 4 May and Offstv Jozsef Kiss, the Hungarian ace of aces with 19 victories, on 19 May.

Sometimes British and Italian claims ran afoul of each other, none more sharply than on 31 July, when Obltn Frank Linke-Crawford, CO of *Flik* 60/J and the fourth-ranking Austrian ace, was killed. In May *Flik* 60/J began replacing its sturdy but relatively sluggish-handling Phönix D Is with Lohner-built Österreichischer Aviatik D Is. Designed by Julius von Berg, the Ö Aviatik or 'Berg' D I was the first fighter in the *Luftfahrtruppen* of entirely Austrian design (the Phönix was essentially a refinement of the Brandenburg D I designed by German Ernst Heinkel). Linke showed what the Berg could do on 10 May by bringing down a Bristol F 2B Fighter as well as a 'Sopwith' that might more likely have been an Italian Hanriot.

The next day Linke-Crawford led an attack on an RE 8, only to be engaged by its Camel escorts of 28 Sqn, during which Capt Percy Wilson claimed an 'Albatros D V' marked with a letter 'L' and Lt O. W. Frayne one marked 'U'. Frayne ran out of fuel on the way home, however, and was injured in the ensuing crash, while Lt E. George Forder, an American from Chicago, was driven down by Linke-Crawford (flying the 'L' marked aeroplane Wilson thought he'd destroyed) and forced to land at *Flik* 60/J's Feltre airfield, where his Camel B2455 was taken intact and himself taken prisoner.

On 1 June Linke-Crawford brought down Camel B2430 of 45 Sqn, its pilot, Lt Earl Hand, by then victor over five opponents, surviving with burns on his hand and back to also become a PoW. Linke claimed two more 'Sopwiths' on 15 and 21 June, and a two-seater, probably another Bristol in Allied lines, on 29 July, bringing his tally to 27.

Although powered by an inline water-cooled engine, the Aviatik D I was unusually manoeuvrable, and in the hands of a skilled veteran like Linke it was the only Austro-Hungarian fighter capable of dogfighting the Camel or a Hanriot HD 1 on even terms. The aeroplane proved to be far less able to

Camel B2455 is shown at *Flik* 60/J's Feltre aerodrome, with the CO, Obltn Frank Linke-Crawford, at right in white trousers, conversing with the captured pilot, Lt E. G. Forder. (Les Rogers via Aaron Weaver)

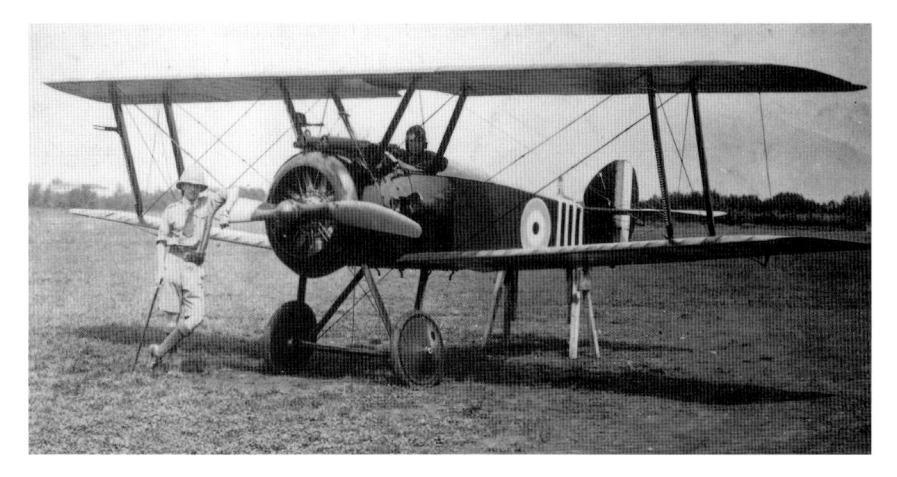

Maj William G. Barker sits in B6313, the most successful Camel of all, accounting for 43 of his 50 victories. It went through several marking changes as it followed him through Nos 28 and 66 Sqns, and when he took command of Bristol F 2B equipped 139 Sqn at Villaverla he brought B6313 with him, initially marking it with the unit's bands and later adding three more. (Greg Van Wyngarden)

endure combat stress than the Camel, however, especially in regard to the empennage. Moreover, Lohner produced its subcontracted Bergs with an even lighter-than-original wing framework, which had already manifested itself in several incidents since May. On 31 July, during another encounter with 45 Sqn, it was Linke's turn to suffer for that inherent weakness.

The RAF, backed by the post-war analysis of 45 Sqn ace Norman Macmillan, attributed Linke's demise to Capt Jack Cottle. While he and the three other Bergs he led that morning did engage three Camels from Macmillan's unit, Linke actually spun down out of the fight due to wing and aileron failure. He managed to regain control of his aeroplane, only to come under attack by two HD 1s flown by Sergente Ciampitti and Caporale Aldo Astolfi of the 81a *Squadriglia*, who claimed that after pursuing it for 20 to 25 minutes they shot the enemy down in flames near Valdobbiadene.

Linke's body was found, with no bullet wounds, near Guia, just east of Valdobbiadene. It is likely that he was credited to all three of his claimants.

Fewer doubts attend Jack Cottle's claim over three Oeffag Albatros D IIIs and a two-seater on 31 August. That day Obltn Friedrich Navratil, the Croatian leader of *Flik* 3/J, attacked a British two-seater and drove it down in Allied lines. At that point, however, four new, inexperienced pilots wandered away, to come under attack by Cottle, leading Lt Mansell R. James and R. G. H. Davis over Campomolon. In short order James killed Ltn d R. Stanislav von Tomicki and Jaroslav Kubelik, while Cottle killed Ltn d R. Josef Pürer (who had been credited with six victories in two-seaters, but had only recently transitioned to single-seaters) and brought down Stabsfeldwebel Otto Förster in Allied lines as a PoW. This brought both Camel pilots' totals to 11, but when Italians handed Pürer's identity card over to Cottle, he thought it bore a resemblance to a favourite cousin who had been serving in the Tank Corps when he was killed at the Somme – and was so disturbed by it that he requested, and was granted, immediate leave.

In September 45 Sqn was transferred to Bettincourt, France, to be equipped with Snipes in order to escort bombers of Independent Force. Only two Snipes turned up before the armistice, but 45's Camels downed seven German two-seaters, including one on 5 November by Cottle, who also downed a Fokker D VII on 3 November. Back in Italy, one flight each of 28 and 66 Sqn marked its Camels with 45 Sqn's dumbbell emblem to deceive the Austro-Hungarians into believing there were still three Camel squadrons as they participated in the last Italian push at Vittorio Veneto.

51

Capt Douglas F. Lapraik (seated seventh from left) and fellow personnel of No 72 Sqn in Mesopotamia pose before a Camel late in 1918. Desert conditions were not kind to rotary engines and although 72 Sqn's 'C' Flight was equipped with rotary engine Bristol M 1C Monoplanes – which were relegated to the 'sideshow' fronts – the Camel (somewhat ironically) was a rarity there. (Andy Kemp)

Italian Gen Armando Diaz had planned to launch his offensive on the anniversary of Caporetto, but stiff Austro-Hungarian resistance in the preliminary stages on 23–24 October and heavy rains that swelled the Piave led him to delay the main assault by 48 hours. That same night, however, the British Tenth Army under Lt Gen Frederick Rudolf Lambart, 10th Earl of Cavan, managed to secure Grave di Papadopoli, an island that established a foothold four-fifths across the river.

In spite of more rain, the Italian preliminary bombardment began on the night of 26 October, but the rains ended the next morning and at 0645hrs Cavan's Tenth Army, aided by skilful Italian boatmen, forged across the Piave and drove back the Austro-Hungarian Fifth Army as it widened the bridgehead.

Oberst Emil Uzelac threw all the aircraft he could muster to attack Allied positions and try to destroy the Piave bridges, but with only 20 aircraft available on 25 October the *Luftfahtruppen* was outnumbered and outclassed as the Allied advance ground on unabated. When not eliminating enemy aeroplanes the Camels of 28 and 66 Sqns were bombing and strafing. In addition nine pilots of 66 Sqn were assigned to destroy the Austro-Hungarian balloon line. Operating in flights of three, they burned 11 in the course of the month. The most successful 'balloon buster' in Italy, Lt Harry King Goode from Nuneaton, Warwickshire, had downed his first kite balloon on 5 August. Flying Camel E7211, he got another on 16 October, shared in another's destruction on the 22nd and then, during Vittorio Veneto, he burned one on the 27th, two on the 28th and one the next day, bringing his overall tally, counting aeroplanes, to 15.

Camel pilots reported about 80 enemy aircraft over the Front on 28 and 29 October, but only five on the 30th, when they shifted their primary mission to bombing and strafing retreating troops and transport. At that point the entire Hapsburg Empire was breaking up and the Austro-Hungarians sued for an armistice. Only the Italians' determination to overrun as much territory as they could before ceasing hostilities delayed its signing, and the general stand-down of forces, until 4 November.

Numerous Camel aces emerged from the fighting over Italy, of which the undisputed champion was Barker, with 43 of his 50 victories scored there – all in B6313, making it the most successful Camel of the war as well as one of the longest-lived, undergoing several changes in markings and configuration as it followed its 'owner' from 28 to 66 and finally 139 Sqn. Another Canadian, Clifford M 'Black Mike' McEwen from Griswold, Manitoba, got all 27 of his victories with 28 Sqn. After being credited with five victories in 1½ Strutters with 45 Sqn over France, Capt Matthew B. Frew from Glasgow, Scotland, added another 18 in Camels over Italy.

The East

British forces had had a presence on the Eastern Mediterranean since Turkey's entry into the war with the Central Powers in November 1914, with the RNAS maintaining a presence in the islands west of the Dardanelles. After the fall of

Serbia in November 1915, British and French forces helped the Serbian army regroup to carry on the fight in Salonika, where it faced the forces of Austria-Hungary, Bulgaria and Germany. Although these combatants were fighting on his country's soil, Greek king Constantine I, whose queen, Sofia, was Kaiser Wilhelm II's sister, maintained a neutralist stand that drove his prime minister, Eleftheios Venizelos, to resign in protest, form an alternative government on Crete, and offer up three divisions comprised of some 20,000 troops willing to fight alongside the Allies in Salonika. This included a contingent of airmen, among whom was naval Lt Aristeides Moraitinis, an observer in the Balkan Wars who had earned his pilot's wings by 1914 and was a founding father of the Greek Naval Flying Corps (NFC). Attached to the RNAS, the Greeks flew with Z Sqn of 2 Wing.

Under Allied pressure, Constantine abdicated on 11 June 1917. With his second son, Alexander, on the throne, Greece declared war on the Central Powers on the 29th and its armed commitment to the Allies swelled to a quarter of a million.

The first Camel in the Aegean arrived at Mudros on the isle of Lemnos on 26 July 1917. The next day Flt Lt John W. Alcock of E Sqn, 2 Wing, flew it during the interception of an enemy seaplane and two escorting fighters, driving one of the latter into the sea. More Camels arrived in August, but on the 12th one attached to D Sqn on Stavros was shot down by enemy fighters. Eight days later another, attached to Z Sqn of 2 Wing, was shot down over Thasos by Ltn Rudolf von Eschwege of *Fl Abt* 30, Flt Cdr C. E. Wood being killed.

On 30 September Alcock, again flying the Camel in company with Sub Flt-Lt Harold T. Mellings in the sector's only Sopwith Triplane, shot down two Albatros W 4 floatplane fighters of the German *Wasserfliegerabteilung* based at Chanak Kale (Canakkale) over Mudros Bay. Flugzeugobermaat Walter Krüger was killed, while his unidentified wingman was taken PoW.

A growing arsenal of replacement Camels were distributed among the various squadrons, a few joining the handful of Bristol Scout Ds and Pups equipping the Greek Z Sqn. In January 1918 they participated in the air battles that raged in the wake of the mining and grounding of the Turkish battlecruiser *Yavuz Sultan Selim* (formerly the *Goeben* and still primarily German-crewed) at Nagara Point.

In one of the first air actions on 20 January, Moraitinis, flying from Imbros, arrived in the area in time to see two Mudros-based Sopwith Baby seaplanes of 6 Wing RNAS try to bomb *Yavuz*, only to come under attack by German fighters, resulting in Flt Sub-Lt William Johnston's Baby going down in flames to Ltn Emil Meinecke of *Fl Abt* 6. Moraitinis, meanwhile, was engaged by ten Turkish aircraft, but was credited with downing three of them. Turkish records later revealed the loss of two 'reconnaissance aeroplanes'.

For the next five days the British and Greeks flew 276 sorties and dropped 15 tons of explosives in an attempt to

Delivered to No 72 Sqn on 27 September, Camel D6447 managed to acquire a nickname by the time it began its brief combat career in November. (Andy Kemp)

destroy *Yavuz*, while German and Turkish aircraft did all in their power to prevent it. Twenty Allied aeroplanes were lost and only two small bomb hits achieved by the night of the 26th, when the Turkish pre-dreadnaught *Torgut Reis* pulled *Yavuz* free and towed it to Constantinople for repairs.

The amalgamation of the RFC and RNAS into the RAF led to a reorganisation of naval units in the Eastern Mediterranean into two sections. Adriatic Group, based at Otranto, included Nos 224 and 225 Sqns, with six Camels assigned between them, and Taranto-based 226 Sqn also with six Camels. The Aegean Group, headquartered at Mudros, included Camel-equipped 220 Sqn at Gliki, 222 Sqn at Imbros and 223 Sqn at Mytilene. By May the British were affording more independence in the conduct of operations to the Greeks, while expanding Z Sqn into four new NFC squadrons: H1 at Thasos, H2 at Mudros, H3 at Stavroupolis and H4 at Mytilene.

Climate in the region largely limited air operations to early morning or late afternoon and opportunities for aerial combat were irregular at best. In July 1918, however, the Turks launched a wave of air attacks on the islands of Mytilene, Chios and Samos. In response, on 13 July Lt Cdr Moraitinis, commanding H2, led a small detachment to Kalloni, on Lesbos. From there he and his six pilots intercepted raiders and struck back at Turkish airfields and installations at Magnesia, Chanak Kale and Smyrna. During this time two Gliki-based 220 Sqn Camels, flown by Flt Sub-Lts E. P. O. Haughton and Robert W. Peel, shot down a German Rumpler on a photoreconnaissance mission on 22 July. At the end of July operations from Kalloni concluded and Moraitinis' detachment rejoined the rest of H2 at Mudros. By the end of the war Moraitinis had flown 185 combat missions – 80 bombing, 27 reconnaissance, 25 maritime patrol and 18 fighter sweeps – during which he engaged in 20 aerial combats and was credited with nine victories. On 22 December 1918, however, he disappeared while flying a Breguet 14 from Thessaloniki to Athens, and is believed to have crashed in the sea somewhere between Halkidiki and Magnesia.

Meanwhile, in Salonika the RFC's Nos 17 and 47 Sqns had to deal with growing German fighter activity as *Jasta* 25 and later *Jasta* 38 were assigned to the sector. In order to protect their reconnaissance aeroplanes both units established fighter flights, which by early 1918 included SE 5as and a few Bristol M 1C monoplanes on their rolls. With the formation of the RAF on 1 April, those two flights were combined into a specialised fighter unit, No 150 Sqn, based at Kirec, Macedonia. On 7 May a flight of Camels joined

Camel D6451 occupies a 72 Sqn hangar at Samarra with SPAD VII A8840 in late September 1918. (Andy Kemp)

the squadron, which in addition to fighter patrols performed light bombing and strafing missions.

The two top-scorers in 150 Sqn, Canadian Capt Gerald Gordon Bell with 13 victories and Lt Charles D. B. Green with 11, attained them all in SE 5as. Its third-ranking ace, Lt Douglas Arthur Davies, got all ten of his in Camel C1566, starting with two Albatros D Vs north of Guevgueli on 12 June; one that fell in flames was probably *Jasta* 38's CO, Obltn Kurt Grasshoff, noted by the Germans as KIA over Predejce.

Canadian Lt Arthur E. deM. Jarvis scored his first two successes in an M 1C with 17 Sqn on 25 and 26 April, his third, an LVG OOC over Hudova, flying a Camel with 150 Sqn on 20 May, and his last four in SE 5as. Lt J. C. Preston got all seven of his victories in Camel D6643, five of them during an intense combat on 18 August; all but one of them achieved in concert with squadronmates. Capt George Cecil Gardiner, who claimed his first two victories in a BE 12 and a de Havilland DH 2 with 47 Sqn, got four more flying Camels with 150 Sqn.

By 30 September 1918, when Bulgaria's surrender effectively ended combat operations in Salonika, 150 Sqn's pilots had added 80 victories to the 36 they had claimed prior to formation. Its strength at that time stood at nine SE 5as, seven Camels, a BE 12 and a Bristol M 1C.

An even more exotic Camel venue was Mesopotamia, whose sandy desert areas on either side of the Tigris and Euphrates rivers may have been amenable to dromedaries but most unpleasant for rotary engine fighters like the Sopwith. In spite of that, rotary engine de Havilland DH 1s and DH 2s, Vickers FB 19s, Bristol M 1C Monoplanes and Nieuport scouts had served in Palestine with No 111 Sqn RAF until joined by Bristol F 2B Fighters and finally a full complement of SE 5as, while the Bristols went over to No 1 Sqn AFC. Farther east, in 'Messpot', No 72 Sqn, formed on 2 July 1917, had arrived in Basra in January 1918 and commenced operations in March.

Reflecting the mixed bag of leftovers that initially equipped its sister units in Palestine, 72 Sqn stationed 'A' Flight at Samarra with SPAD VIIs, SE 5as and a few two-seat DH 4s that were soon withdrawn. 'B' Flight at Baghdad had Martinsyde Elephants, while 'C' Flight at Mirjana had Bristol M 1Cs – excellent rotary engine fighters relegated due to RFC disenchantment with monoplanes in general to sideshows like Salonika, Palestine and Mesopotamia.

On 27 September Camels D6447 and D6451, which had arrived in Mesopotamia on 28 June, were added to 72 Sqn's fighter potpourri. On the same day D6441, D6443, D6445 and D6449 arrived in-theatre, to join the squadron by 1 November.

The Camel came just in time to participate in the campaign's last major action. Since the fall of Baghdad on 11 March 1917, the Mesopotamian Expeditionary Force had been making slow, leisurely progress to the north-west, but that began to change in late September 1918, when Gen Sir Edward Allenby's forces in Palestine flanked the Turks near Megiddo. During that time the greatest contribution by Camels was made by those stationed at Imbros, when the RAF learned of a substantial supply train being assembled south-east of the Dardanelles, slated to reinforce surviving Turkish and German forces regrouping outside of Damascus. A DH 4 and two Camels were dispatched and duly found a large concentration of pack camels assembled 40 miles inland of Tenedos, which they bombed, strafed and ultimately decimated.

With Allenby's success offering the prospect of a general Turkish collapse, Prime Minister David Lloyd George ordered Lt Gen William Raine Marshall to add to the pressure by advancing his army up both the Tigris and Euphrates. Lacking sufficient supplies, Marshall settled for dispatching a cavalry force led by Lt Gen Alexander Cobbe up the Tigris, where it caught and engaged the *Dicle Grubi* (Tigris Group) of the Turkish Sixth Army at Sharqat on 29 October. When a bayonet charge by dismounted British troopers overran his artillery the Turkish commander, Ismail Hakki Bey, called for a ceasefire to end further bloodshed, surrendering on the 30th. Advancing further, the British occupied Mosul on 1 November, bringing the Mesopotamian campaign to an end.

On 31 October an armistice with the Ottoman Empire ended operations in the Eastern Mediterranean and the Middle East. Hellenic naval Squadron H2, however, would continue operating its Camels in Greece's subsequent war against the resurgent Turkish republic until 1923.

Carrier operations

Operating floatplanes from ships dated to the war's first month, but by 1917 the British were starting to operate wheeled aircraft from platforms erected over gun turrets, aided by the oncoming wind into which the ships – or sometimes merely the turrets – were turned. On 21 August 1917 Flt Sub-Lt Bernard Arthur Smart flew a Pup from such a platform on the light cruiser *Yarmouth* to surprise and shoot down the Zeppelin *L23*, which had risen from its base at Tondern to shadow the four cruisers and 15 destroyers of the 3rd Light Cruiser Division. Forced to ditch in the North Sea, Smart was rescued by boats from the destroyer *Prince*, which also salvaged the Pup's engine and machine gun. *L23*'s entire 17-man crew perished with it, leaving the Germans in the dark as to the cause of its demise – a lucky British shell hit was suspected – and the gazetting of Smart's Distinguished Service Order for 'a specially brilliant feat' was intended to keep them unaware of the Grand Fleet's new weapon.

When the aircraft carrier *Furious*, flying the flag of Rear Adm Richard F. Phillimore, joined the Grand Fleet in March 1918, plans were being laid to attack Tondern, an airship base in what is now Denmark, from which Zeppelins were regularly carrying out maritime reconnaissance missions. Equipped with two specially trained flights of 2F1 Camels, which had ropes installed on their upper wing centre sections to facilitate their recovery from the sea in the event of ditching, *Furious* departed Rosyth to carry out the raid, dubbed Operation F5, in late May, only to abort the mission soon after.

In the course of her North Sea patrol that month *Furious*, along with the cruisers *Sydney*, *Melbourne* and *Galatea*, had occasion to send their Camels up to deal with German floatplanes, starting on 1 June when Lt A. C. Sharwood took off from his platform on HMAS *Sydney* in an unsuccessful interception attempt. Finally, on the 19th one of two fighters dispatched from *Furious*, flown by Flt Lt G. Heath, scored the first successful carrier-launched interception and forced an approaching enemy floatplane to land near Heligoland Bight, where it was finished off and its crew captured by the destroyer *Valentine*. On 29 June *Furious* was off the Danish coast for Operation F6, another attempt to bomb Tondern, when Force 6 winds compelled the British to cancel again.

On 16 July, Adm David Beatty ordered Operation F7, yet another strike on Tondern, and *Furious* departed Rosyth the next day. The 19th saw the well-escorted carrier cruising off the Schleswig coast with seven Camels aboard, each carrying two 50lb bombs. First off at 0300hrs was Capt W. D. Jackson, followed by Capt William F. Dickson and Lt N. W. Williams. Twenty minutes later Capt Bernard A. Smart, who had earlier destroyed *L23*, led Capt T. K. Thyne and Lts Stephen Dawson and Walter Albert Yeulett off the deck. A faltering engine caused Thyne to turn back early on and, finding it impossible to land on *Furious*' deck due to the smokestack and bridge remaining in a central position that bisected the flight deck, he ditched and was recovered by a destroyer.

A flight of five Albatros D IIIs had been assigned to Tondern, but its rough field had so damaged the fighters that they were withdrawn on 6 March. Thus Jackson found the base defended only by anti-aircraft guns when he and his flight arrived and dropped their bombs on 'Toska' hangar, containing Zeppelins *L53* and *L60*. Neither airship exploded, but both burned inside the hangar. Engine troubles caused Smart's flight to fall behind him, but all reached the objective and dropped their bombs on 'Tobias' hangar, destroying a balloon therein, as well as destroying two hydrogen cylinders. For all the destruction they wrought, only four Germans were injured in the raid.

Believing they lacked sufficient fuel to rejoin the fleet, three of the Camel pilots flew to Denmark; Capt Jackson landed at Esbjerg and burned his Camel, N6771, before being interned; he was later joined by Williams and Dawson, whose Camels, N6605 and N6823, respectively, were seized by the Danes. All three men later escaped.

Dickson opted to try getting back to *Furious*, and at 0555hrs he ditched his Camel near the destroyer *Violent*, which picked him up. Smart likewise reached the destroyer at 0630hrs, to also be fished from his sinking Camel by *Violent*'s crew.

At 0700hrs the British fleet, judging the time to be past any Camel's endurance, withdrew. Yeulett had also tried to reach it, but failed to locate it before fuel exhaustion forced him down in Ringkobing Fjord. His Camel was washed ashore near Havrig on 24 July and his drowned body turned up at Holmsland four days later. Buried at Havrig, he posthumously received the DFC, a medal also awarded to Jackson, Williams and Dawson. Smart received a bar to his DSO, which also went to Dickson, later to serve as Chief of Defence Staff in 1958–59.

Although its airship hangars were repaired, Tondern ceased regular airship operations, save as an advance base. Costly though it had been in men and aircraft, the raid by *Furious*' Camels was deemed a success and set the precedent for greater carrier operations to come.

Supplementing *Furious* on a dramatically smaller scale was a wooden platform erected on a towed lighter, from which Cdr Charles Rumney Samson

ABOVE LEFT
Even HMS *Furious* was all but impossible to land on in 1918. Ditching and being recovered by crane, as shown with this Ships Camel, was the standard finale to any ship-launched air operation. (Colin A. Owers via Greg Van Wyngarden)

ABOVE RIGHT
Sopwith F1 Camel B3878, still wearing its markings from previous service in No 8 Sqn RNAS, undergoes an experimental ditching with hydrovanes installed on its undercarriage off the Isle of Grain on 9 August 1918. (Colin A. Owers via Greg Van Wyngarden)

proposed to launch 2F1s at sea. His first flight attempt in Camel N6623, using skids as an undercarriage along wooden guide troughs, occurred on 30 May from a lighter being towed at 32 knots, but the aeroplane cartwheeled off the bow and Samson was fortunate to disentangle himself from the wreckage, to be rescued by an accompanying whaler. Samson called for further trials and on 31 July Lt Stuart D. Culley succeeded in getting airborne in a standard wheeled Camel.

The experiment's practical application was not long in coming – on 11 August Culley, in a 2F1 armed with twin Lewis guns fixed above the upper wing and no Vickers, took off from another lighter, towed by destroyer HMS *Redoubt*, ascended to 19,000 feet and shot down Zeppelin *L53* near Terschelling off the Dutch coast. Culley then landed in the water alongside the lighter, whose crew recovered both him and his Camel.

Post-war Camels

Although the state of the art had passed them by, even in the RAF, Camels continued to fly and fight long after the German-accepted armistice silenced the guns on the Western Front – but not at Toulgas in north Russia, where on that very day American soldiers were fighting for their lives against attacking Bolsheviks. Since June 1918 Britain – in an attempt to keep Russia in the war by supporting 'White' armies against the Red government that had ended hostilities with the Germans in March – had landed the first elements of its North Russia Expeditionary Force at Murmansk. In July the seaplane tender *Nariana* landed the first Camel in Russia, to be joined by six more on 12 November.

In addition to Camels operating from Murmansk, Arkhangelsk and Novorossiysk, the type equipped a Slavo-British Group, whose ranks included Russian ace of aces Major Alekandr Kozakov (17 victories) and 'B' Flight of No 47 Sqn, operating in southern Russia under the command of 60-victory Canadian ace Maj Raymond Collishaw. On 28 July 1919, however, word arrived of the decision to withdraw international forces from north Russia and

F THE TONDERN RAID

At 0314 hrs on 19 July 1918, seven Sopwith 2F1 Ships Camels, each carrying two 49-pound Mark III Cooper bombs, left the aircraft carrier *Furious* to attack the German airship base at Tondern. Capt T. K. Thyne aborted due to a faltering engine and, unable to land on *Furious* due to the centrally located smokestack and bridge bisecting its flight deck, ditched and was recovered by a destroyer. Little more than an hour later Capt W. D. Jackson, Capt William F. Dickson and Lt N. W. Williams reached Tondern and bombed the giant 'Toska' hangar, inside of which Zeppelins *L54* and *L60* burned. Twenty minutes later Capt Bernard A. Smart, who had painted his Camel's cowling in aquamarine and white squares for flight identification, bombed 'Tobias' hangar, belatedly followed by Lts Stephen Dawson and Walter Albert Yeulett, resulting in the destruction of a balloon and two hydrogen cylinders. Three pilots, believing themselves unable to rejoin the naval force, landed in Denmark, where Jackson burned his Camel, N6771, but N6605 and N6823, respectively flown by Williams and Dawson, were seized intact. All three internees later escaped. Opting to try returning to *Furious*, Dickson ditched his Camel near the destroyer HMS *Violent* at 0555. Smart ditched near *Violent* at 0630, and was also rescued. Yeulett went missing until his Camel washed ashore near Havrig on 24 July, and his drowned body turned up at Holmsland four days later. Jackson, Williams and Dawson received the DFC as did Yeulett, posthumously, while Smart received a bar to his DSO, and Dickson was also awarded the DSO. Although its airship hangars were repaired, Tondern ceased regular airship operations, save as an advance base. The raid, deemed a success by the Admiralty, set the precedent for greater carrier operations to come.

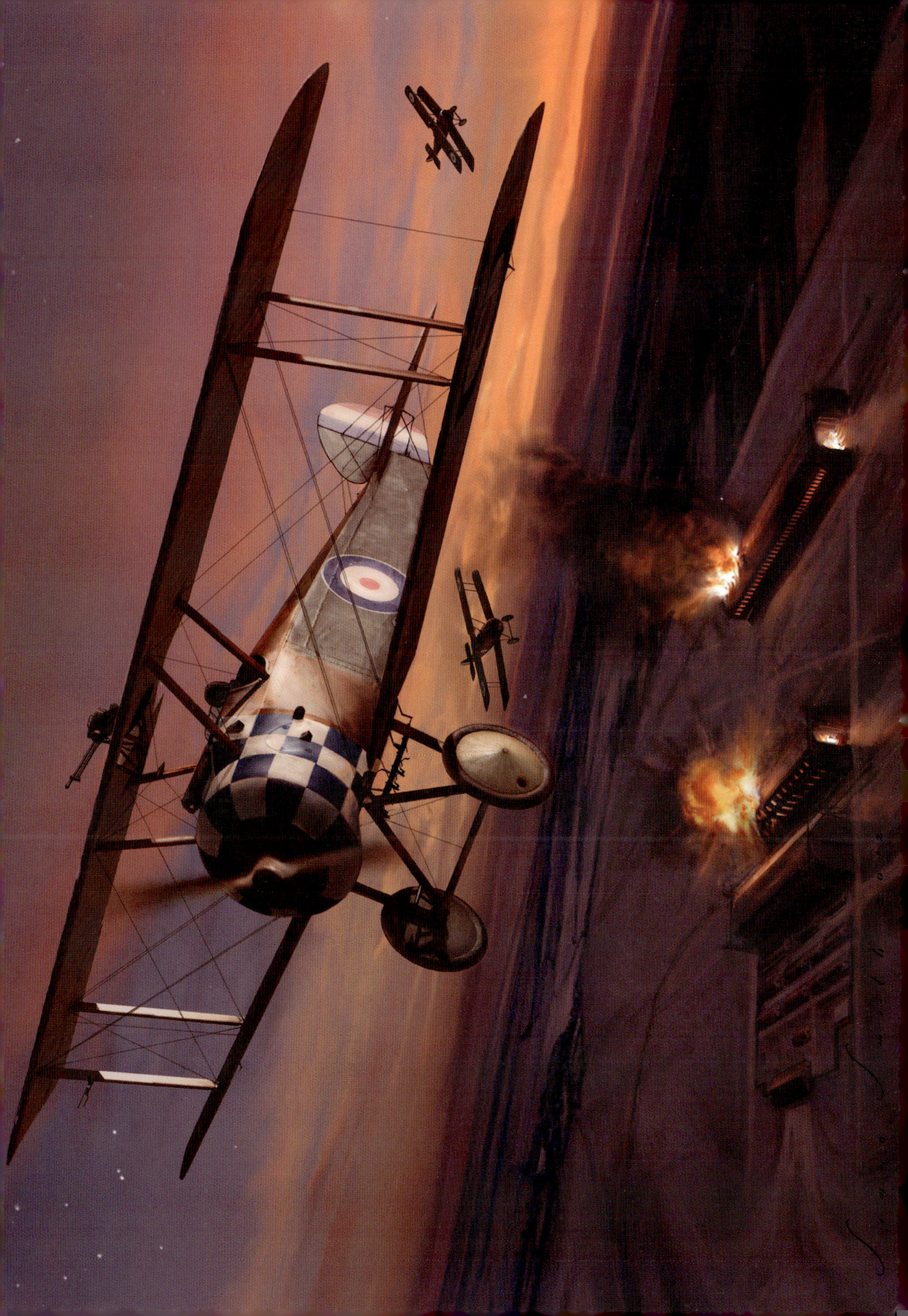

Culley's Camel succeeds in getting airborne from the speeding lighter on 31 July. On 11 August he would put that achievement to practical use by intercepting and destroying Zeppelin *L53* near Terschelling. (Colin A. Owers via Greg Van Wyngarden)

Kozakov became increasingly morose. On 3 August he took off in his Camel, went into a sharp climb, stalled and dived straight into the ground, dying of his injuries shortly after.

In southern Russia No 47 Sqn, first led by Maj Raymond Collishaw (60 victories) and subsequently by Maj George R. M. Reid (9 victories), supported White forces for a much longer time, mainly engaging in ground attack but encountering Bolshevik aircraft often enough to claim 20 of them. The first, a Nieuport crashed on the banks of the Volga River, was claimed in April 1919 by squadron adjutant Capt Marion H. Aten, a Texan who had previously served in No 203 Sqn, but for whom this was the first of an eventual five successes. South African Capt Samuel M. Kinkead was credited with up to ten victories, but was also shot down in May by a 'Fokker triplane', which was more likely the sole Sopwith Triplane the British had sold the Russians and which the Soviets kept flying until 1928, subsequently preserving it at the air museum at Monino. Capt Rowan H. Daly, a Camel veteran of Naval 10, landed nearby, Kinkead squeezed himself over the gun 'hump' and Daly flew him to safety.

Daly eventually added four to the three victories he had scored in World War I, Collishaw claimed an Albatros destroyed and another out of control, and W. Burns-Thompson was credited with two. When the British finally withdrew from Novorossiysk in April 1920, the Camels were lined up at the harbour and crushed by a tank, which then similarly demolished 40 crated DH 9s and was then itself driven into the harbour.

Five or six Camels were delivered to newly resurrected Poland at the end of 1919, but there is no evidence that they saw combat during its war with Soviet Russia the following years, although one, F5234, was brought by its private owner, Kenneth M. Murray, when he joined the American volunteer 7th *Eskadra* 'Kosciuszko' at Lwów. This joined the unit's Oeffag Albatros D IIIs and Ansaldo A 1 Ballilas in ground attack operations against the Bolsheviks from July 1920 through the end of the war.

At least one Camel was still in Polish service at Lwów until 1922, when Lt Col Ludomil A. Rayski took off in it to inspect his air units. The engine failed on take-off, however, and Rayski's face was injured in the subsequent crash.

Breaking away from Russia, Lithuania acquired its first warplane when it captured a Bolshevik-flown F1 Camel and pressed it into service. Estonia acquired 2F1 Ships Camel N6616, which its new air arm flew on anti-Bolshevik operations throughout 1919-20.

Another newly independent Baltic state, Latvia, was presented with seven 2F1 Ships Camels in January and March 1920, but that number was reduced on 2 May when N8137's engine failed. Although the pilot, Ltn Voldemars Skrasins, commander of the 2nd Squadron, managed to restart it, he had lost too much altitude and crashed at Spilve, the first fatality for Latvia's new air arm. The other Camels soldiered on until 1927, when Jekabs Kaire died in a crash at Daugavpils on 14 July and Eduards Lumbergs miscalculated while trying to fly under a bridge near Daugavpils on 6 August and crashed to his death. After that Latvia wrote off its remaining Camels.

A total of 325 Camels were acquired by the United States, of which 143 were slated for frontline use, where combat and operational attrition 'consumed' most of them. The others saw post-war use in the US Army and especially the Navy, with which Lt Cdr Edward O. McDonnell flew one off the No 2 gun turret of the battleship *Texas* while it lay anchored at Guantanamo, Cuba, on 9 March 1919. Few actually saw service and aside from being assigned aboard battleships at least one, flown from Bustleton Field, Pennsylvania, by 1Lt G. B. Newman, US Marine Corps, was involved in a test of flotation gear on 3 December 1919 – only to sink because the air bags failed to inflate. A few American Camels found civilian owners, in the 1920s. Likewise only two of the Camels replaced by Snipes in the RAF entered British civil registry, and one of them crashed on 4 November 1922, killing its owner, Flying Officer W. Burns-Thompson.

Capt Percy Wilson, a seven-victory ace and flight leader of No 28 Sqn, poses beside his Camel, decked out in non-standard décor to celebrate the war's victorious conclusion in Italy. (Les Rogers via Aaron Weaver)

CONCLUSION

With a grand total of 5,695 built, the Sopwith Camel is indisputably one of the most important fighters of World War I. Its handling characteristics, lauded and lamented – sometimes by the same pilots – made it the stuff of legend in themselves, but in combat they may have contributed to one of the aeroplane's most enduring myths. With numerous friends and foes flashing before their eyes in the chaos of a tight-turning, fast-moving dogfight, it is not hard to explain how numbers of aircraft perceived as shot down could be exaggerated in the perception of the Camel pilot who returned. This added up to an official tally – among RFC, RNAS, RAF, AFC and USAS units – of 1,543 aeroplanes destroyed, 120 kite balloons burned, ten enemy aeroplanes captured, and 1,086 driven down out of control, for a grand total of 2,759 victories, a statistic that has since served as the basis of declaring the Camel the most successful fighter of the war – the conflict's 'King of Combat'.

Comparisons with enemy losses in the decades since the armistice tell a different story. Comparing the combat reports of Camels pilots with those of their opponents likewise shows a wide discrepancy between victories, claimed (3,422, hundreds of which involved successes shared by anywhere from two to entire flights of pilots), credited and actually achieved.

Moreover, Camel casualties show the aeroplane to have been far from invincible, with 413 pilots killed in action, 307 PoWs and 189 wounded, in addition to which 385 Camel pilots were killed in accidents. The annihilation of five or six Camels at a time in the war's final months also show that the fighter's fabled manoeuvrability was of limited use against a faster fighter flown by an adversary who knew enough to deny the Camel pilot the

A white-painted Camel of the 41st Aero Sq, USAS, displays the unit emblem, combining a Roman numeral 'V' for the 5th Pursuit Group with a Camel, since the group's other squadrons used SPAD VIIs and XIIIs. Formed on 15 November 1918, four days after the armistice, the 5th Pursuit Group performed occupation duties in Germany until September 1919. (Greg Van Wyngarden)

opportunity to bring his principal advantage into play. To put Allied overclaiming in perspective, though, it is only fair to note that for every Camel brought down there is an account like those of Alfred Koch or George Vaughn, of an aeroplane so badly shot-up that it was actually credited to its assailant as a kill, but which in fact managed to bring its pilot over Allied lines or even his own aerodrome, alive to fight another day.

If it was less than the world-beater of myth, however, the nimble, simple, durable Camel remains a formidable weapon with a vast record of documented accomplishments by any standard. It may not have ended Manfred von Richthofen's career, but it shot down a great number of his disciples, starting with Kurt Wolff and including his brother, Lothar (wounded on 13 March 1918 by either a Camel of No 73 Sqn, a Bristol F 2B of No 62 Sqn, or both). It also dispatched several Austro-Hungarian aces, although some of their demises face counter-claims by Italian Hanriot HD 1 pilots, loath to be either denied or dismissed.

Besides its much-publicised frontline activities, the versatile Camel destroyed airships, burned kite balloons, intercepted night raiders, took off from ships to bomb faraway objectives and dutifully carried out the 'dirty job' of bombing and strafing ground targets in the face of withering small arms fire. It served as a test-bed for numerous innovations and helped advance the

Sopwith-built F1 Camel B6291, powered by a Gnome engine, clears a hangar roof during a demonstration flight at the Javier Arango Collection, Paso Robles, California, in October 2011. (Jon Guttman)

development of carrier warfare, setting precedents that would be fully realised in the next conflict.

No, the Camel was never a world-beater. Even its status as the supreme dogfighter of its time will forever be debated against its classic – and equally overrated – counterpart, the Fokker Dr I. It does, however, still have ample solid merits on which to stand tall as one of the great warplanes of World War I. Seven original Camels are known to be extant today. An authentic F1 Camel survived in Britain, which, with the serial F6314 and 65 Sqn markings, is now on display at the RAF Museum in Hendon. Camel B7280, whose pilots were credited with 11 victories in the course of its career, is preserved at the Polish Aviation Museum. A Camel is at Belgium's Brussels Air Museum, another is in New Zealand and B6291, restored by British Aerospace, was purchased and is currently kept flying by the Javier Arango Collection at Paso Robles, California. Of the 2F1 Ships Camels, Lt S. D. Culley's historic Beardmore-built 2F1 N6812 has been preserved in the Imperial War Museum, while N8156, which was acquired by Royal Canadian Air Force until 1924 and last flew in June 1967, is on display in the Canada Aviation and Space Museum at Ottawa. In more recent years, aviation enthusiasts around the world have built replicas of varying authenticity to experience – and hopefully master – the peculiar flight characteristics of Sopwith's 'fierce little beast'.

FURTHER READING

Bowyer, Chaz, *Sopwith Camel, King of Combat*, Glassney Press, Oxford (1978)
Bruce, J.M., *Sopwith Camel*, Arms and Armour Press, London (1989)
Bruce, J.M., *The Sopwith Fighters*, Arms and Armour Press, London (1986)
Bruce, J.M., *The Sopwith Camel F.1*, Profile Publications Ltd., Leatherhead, Surrey (1965)
Franks, Norman, Bailey, Frank & Duiven, Rick, *The Jasta War Chronology*, Grub Street, London (1998)
Lanoe, Donald J., interviewer, 'Diary of a Camel Pilot: Lt Robert J McLeod, No 3 Sq, RAF', *Cross & Cockade (USA) Journal*, Vol. 5, No. 1, Spring 1964, pp. 30-38.
Macmillan, Norman, *Offensive Patrol, The Story of the RNAS, RFC and RAF in Italy*, 1917-18, Jarrolds Publishers Ltd, London (1973)
Revell, Alex, *British Single-Seater Fighter Squadrons on the Western Front in World War I*, Schiffer Publishing Ltd., Atglen, PA (2006)
Rimell, Raymond Laurence, *Zeppelin!* Conway Press Ltd, London (1984)
Rochford, Leonard H., *I Chose the Sky*, William Kimber & Co Ltd, London (1977)
Shores, Christopher, Franks, Norman & Guest, Russell, *Above the Trenches*, Grub Street, London (1990)
Strähle, Paul, 'The War Diary of a German Aviator, 11 Aug 1917-22 April 1918,' *Cross & Cockade (International) Journal*, Vol. 11, No. 4, p.158.
Vaughan, David K., editor, *Letters from a War Bird: The World War I Correspondence of Elliott White Springs*, The University of South Carolina Press, Columbia, SC, 2011, pp.179-180.
Waugh, Colin, 'A Short History of 70 Squadron, RFC/RAF 1916-1919,' *Cross & Cockade (USA) Journal*, Vol. 20 No. 4, Winter 1979, pp. 311-312.
Whetton, Douglass, 'Yesterday's Memories – Recollections of Captain Cedric N. Jones, 70 Squadron RFC,' *Cross & Cockade (Great Britain) Journal*, Vol. 1, No. 3, Autumn 1970, p. 54.

INDEX

References to illustrations and plates are in **bold**. Captions to plates are shown in brackets.

Admiralty, the 6, 8, 13, 30
AFC *see* Australian Flying Corps
aircraft, British: Bristol 36, 37, 40, 50, 53, 55; de Havilland 17, 34, 55; floatplanes 56–8; Nieuport 38, 55, 60; RE 8; 44, 46; Sopwith 1½ Strutter 5–6, 8, **11** (10), 23, 32, 52; Sopwith Baby 5, 53; Sopwith Comic 4, **11** (10), **19** (18), **22**, 23–5; Sopwith Dolphin **27** (26), 38, 40; Sopwith Pup 4, 8, 9, 12, 30, 33, 53, 56; Sopwith Scout 6, 8; Sopwith Snipe 28, 37, 42, 51; Sopwith Tabloid 4–5; Sopwith Triplane 8, 9; *see also* Sopwith Camel
aircraft, French: 8, **27** (26), 33
aircraft, German 12; Albatros **7** (6), 8, 16, **19** (18), **27** (26), 32, 33, 34, 35, 37, 43, 44, 45, **47** (46), 48, 50, 51, 53, 55, 57, 60; DFW 42, 43, 44; Fokker 25, **27** (26), 28, 33, 34, 36, 37, 39, 40–1, 42; G IV 22, 44; Gotha 4, **11** (10), **19** (18), 22, 23, 24, 25; Halberstadt 34, 39; LVG 8, 42, 55; triplanes 33–4, 36–7; Zeppelin-Staaken 23, 25
aircraft, Italian 43, 44, 49, 50, 62
airships 31; Zeppelin 4, **11** (10), 22, 56, 57, **59** (58)
Alexander, King of Greece 53
Allenby, Gen Sir Edward 55
Amiens, battle of 40–1
Apps, 2Lt Gordon F. M. **45**, **47** (46)
armistice, the 25, 26, 28, 31, 42, 51, 58
Ashfield, R.J. 5, 8
Australian Flying Corps (AFC) 37, **38**, **39**, 40, 42
Austro-Hungarians 43, 48, 49, 50–1, 52, 62; *see also Fliegerkompagnien (Fliks)*
awards 22, 24, 33, 48, 49, 57, **59** (58)

balloons 37, 40, 43, 52, 57
Baltic States 60–1
Banks, Lt Charles Chaplin **19** (18), 22, 23
Baracca, Francesco 49–50
Barker, Capt William G. **7** (6), 36, 43, 50, **51**, 52
Belgian Air Force (*Aviation Militaire Belge*) **27** (26), **44**, **45**
Bentley, Walter Owen 10, 13–14
Berg, Julius von 50
Bey, Ismail Hakki 56
Billik, Ltn Paul 37
Birks, 2Lt Gerald A. **45**, **47** (46), **49**, 50
bombing raids 22, 23–5, 43, 49
Boulton & Paul Ltd 12, 14, **17**, 25, 28
Brumowski, Hptm Godwin 45

Carpenter, Capt Peter **45**, 48
Clayton & Shuttleworth 13, 18, **27** (26), 43
Cobby, Capt Arthur H. **39**
Collett, Capt Clive Franklyn **19** (18)
Colley, George E. 16
Constantine I, King of Greece 53
Constantinesco, George 16–17
Cottle, Capt Jack 51
Cremers, *Adj* Léon **45**
Culley, Lt Stuart D. **27** (26), 31, 58, **60**

Dawson, Lt Stephen 57, **59** (58)
Dhanis, Robert 44
Diaz, Gen Armando 52
Dickson, Capt William F. 57, **59** (58)
dogfighting 25, 34, 37, 38, 50, 61

Eastern Mediterranean 52–6
Ely, Eugene 29
engines 5, 6, 8, 9, 10, 12, 13, 16, 17, 21, 26, 28, 29, 38

Flanders 4, **5**, 33, 38
Fliegerkompagnien (Fliks) 45, **47** (46), 48, 50, 51
France 8, 9, 12, 13, 24, 25, 29, 43, 51

German Air Force *see Jasta*
Greece 53–5
ground attacks 34–5, 60

Hackwill, Capt George H. **19** (18), 23
Hand, 2Lt Earl McNabb 44, 45, 50
Hanstein, Ltn Ludwig **19** (18), 36
Hapsburg Empire 49, 52
Hawker, Harry 6, 8, 9, 28
Heiden, Uffz Walter **19** (18), 23
Home Defence (HD) **19** (18), 22, 23, 24, 25, 36
Hubbard, Capt Will **27** (26)

Italian Air Force 43, 44, 51
Italy 34, 36, 43–52

Jackson, Capt W. D. 57, **59** (58)
Jasta (German Air Force): 1; 43, 44; 10; 25, 33, 34; 11; 32, 33, 34, 37; 17; 36; 18; 36; 23b; **19** (18), **37**; 38; 54, 55; 39; 43, 44, 45, 46; Boelcke 35, 36, 41, 42; *Jagdgeschwader* 33, 40, 41; *Marine Feld Jastas* (MFJ) **27** (26), 41–2
Jerrard, 2Lt Alan **45**, 48–9

Kaiserschlacht, der (German Spring Offensive) 36–7
Keys, Lt R. E. 31, **33**
Kissenberth, Ltn Otto **19** (18), **37**
Knotts, 2Lt Howard C. **27** (26)
Koch, 2Lt Alfred 35, 62

Lapraik, Capt Douglas F. **52**
Linke-Crawford, Obltn Frank 45, 50, 51
Lloyd George, David 55
Lockhart, 2Lt William S. **32**

MacLaren, Capt Donald Roderick **40**, 42
Macmillan, Capt Norman 33, 51
Malik, 2Lt Hardit Singh **7** (6), 36
Martlesham Heath 9, 10, 13, 14, 28, 30
Maund, Flt Sub-Lt Hugh B. **19** (18)
McLeod, Lt Robert J. 21, 40–1
Mesopotamia 4, **52**, 55–6
Mitchell, Lt James H. 36, 44, 45, 46, 48
Monte Tomba (Italy) **47** (46)
Moraitinis, Lt Aristeides 53, 54
Murlis-Green, Maj Gilbert W. 22, 23, 24

night-time operations 22–3, 24–5, **28**

Palestine 55
parachutes 17, 25
Passchendaele, battle of 33–6
Patzelt, Obltn Karl **47** (46), 50
pilots 4, 6, 8, 9, 10, 17, 18, 20–1, 23, 42; American 38–40; training of 25, 26, 28
Poland 55
prisoners of war (PoW) 25, **27** (26), 36, 37, 40, 41, 50

Quintin-Brand, Capt Christopher J. 22, 24

Ralston, 1Lt Orville A. 38–9
Richthofen, Rittm Manfred von ('Red Baron') 33, 34, 37, 62
Rochford, Flt Sub-Lt Leonard H. 12, 13–14
Royal Air Force (RAF) 13, 14, 49, 51, 54; 3 Sqn 21, **27** (26); 11 Sqn 36; 46 Sqn 33; 47 Sqn 58, 60; 56 Sqn 33; 65 Wing 12, 38; 70 Sqn 33; 72 Sqn 55; 84 Sqn 39; 85 Sqn 38; 111 Sqn 55; 150 Sqn 54–5; 152 Sqn 25; 201 Sqn 17; 203 Sqn 17; 208 Sqn 25; 209 Sqn 40
Royal Flying Corps (RFC) 5, 6, 8, 9; 3 Sqn 12, **20**, 37, 40; 17 Sqn 54; 23 Sqn 35; 28 Sqn **7** (6), 34, 35, 36, 43, 44, 45, 50, 52; 34 Sqn 43; 42 Sqn 43, 44; 43 Sqn 36–7; 45 Sqn 33, 34, 43, 44, 46, 50, 51, 52; 46 Sqn 12, 37, 42; 47 Sqn 54, 55; 54 Sqn 40; 56 Sqn 34, 41; 57 Sqn 34; 60 Sqn 28, 34; 65 Sqn **16**, 40, 41; 66 Sqn 43, **45**, **47** (46), 48, 52; 70 Sqn 12, **19** (18), 32, 33, 35, 36, 41; 71 Sqn **38**; 72 Sqn **52**; 73 Sqn 37; 201 Sqn 40; 204 Sqn 40, 41; 209 Sqn 37; 210 Sqn 42; 213 Sqn 41, 42; Testing Sqn 9–10
Royal Naval Air Service (RNAS) 5, 6, 8, 30, 52–3, 54; 3 Sqn 12, 13; 4 Sqn 12; 9 Sqn **5**, 17; 10 Sqn **19** (18)
Royal Navy 29, 30, 31
Russia 4, 58, 60–1

Serbia 52–3
ships **34**, 56–8; *Furious*, HMS 30, 31, 56, 57, **59** (58)
Smart, Flt Sub-Lt Bernard Arthur 56, 57, **59** (58)
Smith, Herbert 5, 8
Sopwith Camel **19** (18), **27** (26); armament of **11** (10); design of 16–17; development of 8–10, 12–14; flying of 4, 9, 12, 18, 20–1, 31, 39–40; monoplanes 28, **30**; museum pieces **27** (26), 60, 63; night-fighting 4, 22–3, 24–5, **28**; paintwork **19** (18), **21**, **22**, **24**, 38, **59** (58); performance of 5, 6, 8, 15–16, 20–1; post-war operations 58, 60–1; reputation of 32, 61–3; retirement of 43; Ship 4, **8**, 12, 13, **27** (26), 29–31, **32**, **34**, **57**, **59** (58), **60**; trench fighters 29; two-seater **11** (10), 21, 25–6, 28; *see also* engines; weaponry
Sopwith, Thomas 4, 5, 6, 8, 9, 30
Springs, 1Lt Elliott White 38, 39
Strähle, Ltn Paul **7** (6), 36, 41
Sykes, Capt Ronald 17–18, 20–1

Thomsen, Ltn Friedrich von **19** (18), 23
Thyne, Capt T. K. 57, **59** (58)
Tondern (Denmark) 56–8, **59** (58)
Trenchard, Maj Gen Hugh 6, 12, 28
Trollope, Lt John Lightfoot **35**, 37
Turkey 52–6

US Army Air Service (USAS) 14, 40, 61, **62**; 17th Aero Sqn 12, **27** (26), 38, 39, 41; 148th Aero Sqn 12, 38, 41; 185th Aero Sqn **24**, 25

Van der Voordt, 1E Sgt Maj Jean **27** (26)
Vaughn, 1Lt George A., Jr 39–40, 62
Venizelos, Eleftheios 53
Voss, Ltn Werner 33–4

weaponry: bombs **11** (10), **16**, 17, 24, 34–5, 57; cannons 25; guns 5, 8, 9, 10, **17**, 20, 23, 28, 29, 30, 58; interrupter gears 5, 8, 12; rockets 30
weather conditions 52, 54, 56, 57
Webb, Capt Noel W. 32, 33
Western Front 22, 32–43, 45, 58
Wilhelm II, Kaiser 53
William Beardmore & Co Ltd 13, 30
Williams, Capt Thomas Frederic 'Voss' 34, 44
Williams, Lt N. W. 57, **59** (58)
Wilson, Capt Percy 50, **61**
Wolff, Ltn Kurt 33, 34, 62
Woollett, Capt Henry Winslow 36

Yeulett, Lt Walter Albert 57, **59** (58)